MEGA FORCES

SIGNS AND WONDERS OF THE COMING CHAOS

TEXE MARRS

Living Truth Publishers
Austin, Texas

To the memory of my much-loved father,
William Troy, who is now with the Lord,
and to my mother, Josephine, whose
Christian love and caring has meant
so much to me.

Published 1988 by:
        Living Truth Publishers
        8103 Shiloh Court
        Austin, Texas 78745

Originally published as *RUSH TO ARMAGEDDON,*
Tyndale House Publishers/Living Books, 1987

Scripture quotations are from the King James Version
of The Holy Bible.

Library of Congress Catalog Card Number: 88-80305
ISBN 0-9620086-0-5
©1987 by Texe Marrs
All rights reserved.
Printed in the United States of America.

CONTENTS

PART THREE
War Fever

CONCLUSION

A SPECIAL MESSAGE FROM TEXE MARRS

What is in *your* immediate future? What lies
in store for your loved ones? The signs and
wonders of today's prosperous and shining high
tech world deceptively suggest that mankind has
a radiant and glorious future, full of hope and
promise. Scientists and technologists point to
such imminent advances as new miracle drugs,
thinking robots, living computers, and
bioengineered babies as proof of the dawning of
a new era of greatness and renaissance for man.
The New Age religion even proposes that men
and women of "higher consciousness" *who reject
Jesus Christ* will become gods: immortal super-
beings capable of incredible magical feats.

However, behind the facade of modern prosperity and progress—and veiled underneath the
New Age deception—lies a far different story of
a bleak and dreadful future. Stockpiles of nuclear
and chemical weapons continue to mount up.
Shrewd but atheistic Soviet leader Mikhail
Gorbachev speaks of peace and disarmament but
continues to prepare his nation for war with new
space killer systems, psychic warfare weapons
and hideous new biotechnological (germ warfare)
armaments.

Ominously, science is giving today's dictators
advanced tech tools that will surely be used by
the coming Antichrist to control, persccute and
torture Christians and other resisters of his One

World Religion and Government. Such tools include the development of monstrous nightmare machines to torture men's minds, the use of lasers and computers for surveillance, and the invention of fantastic new biochips that can be inserted into the human brain to make a person believe in any false doctrine and act exactly the way despotic rulers wish.

The Bible prophesies a coming period of utter chaos and a tribulation period of terribly malignant proportions. This savage but brief time of woe will be accompanied by a climactic nuclear World War III, referred to simply as *Armageddon*. The signs and wonders of today's high tech society are, in fact, those prophesied in our Bible. We are rushing on an unstoppable, fast-plunging roller coaster toward Armageddon. The vast majority cannot escape their destiny. They will perish in their sins.

The Bible does, however, offer hope. Magnificent hope. It tells us that God's only begotten Son, Jesus Christ, willingly sacrificed himself on the cross. He died for my sins and your sins. Now He lives and is our Judge. In Him lies peace and happiness, joy and eternal security. Do you know Him as your personal saviour? Are you prepared to meet Him?

PREFACE

Powerful forces swirl around mankind today, forces destined to bring about a profound change in both our physical and spiritual worlds. Man cannot avoid these forces any more than he could avoid being brought forth into this world and having breath entered into his lungs.

As we survey the world around us, we recognize a number of malignant and dark forces opposing God and his Word. These forces have seized upon science and technology as prime tools for the exploitation and conquest of souls.

The age of high technology has arrived with magnum force. Computers, telecommunications satellites, lasers, artificial life, and other mind-boggling breakthroughs are transforming our material lives and even the way we think and act. John Sculley, chief executive officer at Apple Computer Corporation, recently remarked that technological advances are occurring so rapidly that "we're going through a time compression—almost a time warp."

The marvels of technology and the increasing reservoir of intellectual knowledge offer us the promise of affluence and material possessions. However, the wonders of technology have not infused men and women with happiness. Worse, new technological advances now make it possible for mankind to plunge into a catastrophic conflict in which bioengineered toxins, nuclear weapons, laser death rays, and other instruments of war cause tragic destruction.

Throughout this book, I will discuss new developments in technology and new theories in science, explaining their impact (and potential impact) on the Christian church and the world at large. Today's Christians are being presented monumental challenges. Scientific and technological discoveries on the horizon are likely to encourage humanist advocates in their irresponsible claims that the Christian faith and the Bible are fundamentally flawed and irrelevant.

Already a deluge of scientific reports seek to convince us that psychic abilities can enable man to possess Godlike powers, or that worldwide computer networking will produce a universal mind. Meanwhile, a growing legion of scientists proposes that man's brain is evolving toward a superhuman intelligence capacity, or even "God" status. It is suggested that the Second Genesis—man's creation of genetically engineered laboratory life and robots with artificial intelligence— makes him a cocreator with God. A prominent authority on science has boldly announced that if man's current quest to locate or communicate with extraterrestrials from outer space is successful, the death knell will sound for Christianity.

At the same time, Christianity is also under attack

by a coalition of eminent scientists and intellectuals who have boldly announced the dawning of a New Age in which science, technology, and man are exalted and enthroned while God, his Son Jesus, and his Word are debased. These determined opponents of Christianity propose a new, "scientific" world church, founded on the idea that man is on the way to becoming a god. Many of these opponents are dedicated to the practice of Eastern religions, sorcery, the occult, and the glorification of the material world.

Serving as the cornerstone of this ideology is an unholy alliance of science and religion. Sir Julian Huxley, one of its earliest advocates, called this a "religion without revelation." Such a religion, said Huxley, can win universal acceptance because "this new, better religion would be based on truths like those of science that could be adjusted to meet new knowledge, discoveries, and insights."[1]

Huxley and others use the term *Evolutionary Humanism* to describe the new religion because of its focus on the individual rather than God. According to Huxley, "The well-developed, well-patterned, individual human being is, in a strictly scientific sense, the highest phenomenon of which we have knowledge, and the variety of individual personalities is the world's highest riches."

Another great challenge confronting Christianity—indeed all of humanity—is the issue of nuclear armaments and other military weaponry. In reviewing the panorama of weapons employing the incomparable technological wizardry of the computer age, we cannot help but feel disoriented and perplexed. In only a few decades, the superpowers (the U.S. and the Soviet

Union) have worked at a frenzied pace to build inventories of such lethal instruments of war as Star Wars defense systems (called SDI—Strategic Defense Initiative—by the U.S. Department of Defense), laser and particle beam weapons, neutron bombs, robot craft, huge missile-carrying submarines, and growing stocks of chemical and biological munitions. Even mind powers—psychic weapons—are being harnessed and prepared for conflict.

Tragically, the world's governments have demonstrated few signs of being able to resolve issues peacefully. As I write this, much of the world's population is at war and terrorism is a plague across the globe. Fear is rampant that terrorists may soon shock the world by exploding a small, mobile nuclear device or, perhaps, by poisoning a city's water system with chemicals or biological toxins.

Who can question the fact that, since the days of Adam, man has done a horrible job of controlling the vast store of knowledge he has acquired? In these final years of the second millennium since Christ's birth, God must look down on his creation with dismay. Nations bristle with armaments while many scientists and technologists boast that man is himself divine. The scientific and technical achievements and the affluence that should cause man to praise the God that makes all things possible have, instead, become stumbling blocks to man's salvation.

But as we begin our study of man's abuse of technology and science and his seemingly stubborn march toward self-destruction, we should keep in mind that there *is* an alternative. Thousands have already found it. That alternative is a life centered on worship of the loving Creator, not worship of man and his technological wonders. This devotion to God brings peace in the midst of global turmoil.

Christians should be alarmed over what they see in the world here below, but we can also take to heart the uplifting words of Paul in Romans 8:35, 37-39:

> Who shall separate us from the love of Christ? Shall tribulation, or distress, or persecution, or famine, or nakedness, or peril, or sword? Nay, in all these things we are more than conquerors through him that loved us. For I am persuaded, that neither death, nor life, nor angels, nor principalities, nor powers, nor things present, nor things to come, nor height, nor depth, nor any other creature, shall be able to separate us from the love of God, which is in Christ Jesus our Lord.

Texe Marrs
Austin, Texas

PART ONE

The God of Forces and the Wizards of Invention

ONE
WHO NEEDS GOD?

"Who needs God?" my friend asked. "There is little that man cannot do, once he sets his mind to it. Look at our space shuttle and the computer."

Sitting in the living area of this man's extraordinarily beautiful home, I could understand—though not agree—with his sentiments. My friend seemingly had everything: a Ph.D. education, a high-paying job in a scientific field, and a good share of all the luxuries and comforts that come with affluence in America. But still, he had reservations—and fears. "Of course, this could all go up in flames," he said, a sigh in his voice, "if someone in Moscow or Washington decides to plunge the world into nuclear holocaust."

The vast majority of people in today's world are much like my friend. They profess to be self-sufficient and that a personal God is an unnecessary contrivance. The wealth and affluence of the commercial, scientific age in which we live provides all of us with goods and conveniences not enjoyed even by the greatest of ancient kings. And science and high technology hold out the promise of far greater things to come.

Yet, deep inside the wells of their consciousness, people are alarmed. Even as they fill up their daily lives with electronic pleasures and digital thrills and accumulate more and more goods, most recognize that something is not right in the world. Insecurity is the plague of modern society.

Gordon Childe, the British archaeologist, historian, and anthropologist, was one who professed little need for God. His acclaimed 1936 book *Man Makes Himself* outlined the origin and progress of man and denied the Bible's story of creation.[1] Childe's works are the basis for much of modern scientific thought and are often cited by those who deny the Bible's teachings that God created man in his image. Childe held that man himself was responsible for becoming "civilized" and that man deserves great credit for taking command of the skies and the seas and for unraveling many of the secrets of nature.

In a 1983 foreword to *Man Makes Himself*, Professor Glyn Daniel of Cambridge University in England stated:

> There was no God or any other form of supernatural inspiration in Childe's view of human history; the emphasis was on the technical development of man and the accumulation of new inventions and new discoveries. The progress of man was not a progress from evil to good: it was a development of material culture which enabled the population of the world to grow and prosper.

According to Professor Daniel, Childe was deemed by many to be a Marxist and, like many other Marxists in and out of Russia, he emphasized that technology alone has brought man progress and raised him from the status of a savage. This is no doubt the view of millions today—scientists and laymen—who hold that mankind's hope lies in continued scientific progress.

In 1957 Dr. Gordon Childe died, and the news of his death came as a great shock to the world of archaeology. His friends said that in his later years the brilliant scientist had become increasingly disillusioned with life. He told a close colleague, "I know a two thousand-foot cliff in Australia. I intend to jump off it." In his writings is found this sad statement: "I have lost faith in my old ideals. There is nothing more I want to do . . . nothing I feel I ought and could do." And so, says Professor Daniel, "He went up the Blue Mountains, put down his spectacles, and jumped."

THE PARADOX

It is a paradox that as man's knowledge increases and his science brings material progress, he has no security and is increasingly alarmed at what tomorrow will bring. We all know that gleaming skyscrapers and technological wonders can be reduced to rubble within minutes by the blast of nuclear weapons. Though we are in the midst of an information and knowledge explosion, and riches abound throughout the Western world, a great many people are, like Gordon Childe, disillusioned with life. The emptiness of everyday existence leads thousands to desperately seek after worldly pleasures and thrills, including drugs and alcohol, sex and crime, while an increasing number opt for suicide. The most affluent societies—the U.S., Sweden, and Switzerland, for example—have alarmingly high suicide rates.

Why this paradox? Why, as society becomes satiated with possessions and as high technology brings to mankind manifold wonders, are people unsatisfied and unfulfilled? Christians know the answer. *It is God alone who brings peace and lasting contentment.* Astounding developments in modern technology have brought us lightning-fast, powerful computers, vast television and communications networks, robots with artificial computer intelligence, rapid means of travel, space exploration, and unbelievable progress in medicine. But science and technology have not brought mankind inner peace and happiness.

Even though spectacular technological achievements occur rapidly, the level of global human misery and immorality continues to increase. This puts the lie to the contention of scientists that science is the key to all of man's problems. The failure of science and its cousins, psychology and sociology, to improve the quality of our world and to stem the flood tide of crime and immorality is a stark reminder to God's people that without spiritual wisdom earthly knowledge has no value.

The Apostle Paul told us that in the last days would come perilous times:

> For men shall be lovers of their own selves, covetous, boasters, proud, blasphemers, disobedient to parents, unthankful, unholy, without natural affection, trucebreakers, false accusers, inconti-

nent, fierce, despisers of those that are good.
(2 Tim. 3:2, 3)

Those times certainly seem to have arrived, and we
are feeling their effect even in our churches. In disregard of the Bible's admonition against homosexuality
(1 Cor. 6:9), many churches ordain gays and lesbians
to the ministry. Some versions of our Bible have been
rewritten by liberal church authorities to produce a sex-
neutral vocabulary in which the terms Lord and Father
are missing.

Meanwhile, some ecumenical church groups in the
United States send money and aid to international terrorist and pro-Communist groups abroad, and congregations seem unable or unwilling to put a stop to these
outrages. The churches seem morally confused, just as
Western society as a whole seems disoriented. Technological expertise has done nothing to increase our faith
in moral absolutes.

THE HIGH-TECH EXPLOSION

The biblical prophets foresaw that, in the last days, the
fast-paced world would see fantastic technological
progress. One prophet who predicted this was Daniel:
"Many shall run to and fro, and knowledge shall be increased" (Dan. 12:4). This prophesy has certainly been
borne out, for rapid transportation now enables many
to "run to and fro," and knowledge is increasing at an
incredible rate. We are told that 90 percent of all the
scientists who ever lived are alive today, and that the
educational level of the masses is higher than at any
time in human history. If knowledge alone brought

happiness, we would be an immensely joyous people. But without God's wisdom, knowledge is barren. We note that Paul prophesied (2 Tim. 3:7) that in the last days intellectuals and learned men would nevertheless *not* be imbued with truth and wisdom. Instead, men will be "ever learning, and never able to come to the knowledge of the truth."

Alas, increased knowledge does not lead to truth or happiness. In the year 2000, though miracle drugs will make us healthier and computerized homes and working robots may free us from drudgery, mankind will not be happy. In fact, the danger is that technology may lead to enslavement and new barbarism.

Science has a dark side that must be faced. Many technological advances have tended to dehumanize man and made him prey to evil and corrupt leadership. Elizabeth C. Hirschman, professor at New York University, has said people "are being increasingly socialized to learn from, talk to, and create with machines rather than with other humans." Further, she observes that people so taught may lack the mental power of analysis and may someday be unable to sufficiently understand the significance of political and social events. "When and if this time arrives," she says, "[George Orwell's] *1984* will be here."[2]

In the digital society, unless he accepts and trusts in God, man is alone. Technology breeds impersonal behavior. We educate ourselves with a machine (the computer), acquire pleasure from a machine (the TV), obtain and spend money by machine (automatic tellers), and machines do our work (robots), rendering many human workers unemployable. The danger is that man himself will become a machine. He will become a waste product, expendable to those in power.

TECHNOLOGY AND IMMORALITY

We know that technology can be wrongly used. The same laser that miraculously restores sight to the blind can also be used to blind enemy soldiers in combat by permanently searing their optic nerves (see chapter 10). The same computer that permits a disabled amputee to productively work at home can also be used to ferret out and destroy innocent men and women who defy the dictates of a future Antichrist.

Technology in itself is ethically neutral, being neither good nor evil. Used wisely, technology makes our lives easier, helps to free us from debilitating disease, and permits us unparalleled free time. For example, new computer-controlled wheelchairs are a godsend for crippled adults, and advances in biotechnology yield wonderful results to thousands of victims of disease as miracle drugs are formulated using bioengineering techniques. More benefits of technology include the success of the Space Lab, which promises new manufacturing techniques for improved drugs, and the use of surgical lasers in the operating room to heal detached eye retinas, vaporize deadly cancer cells, and blast away obstructions from clogged arteries.

These technological advances benefit mankind, and we know that God is involved in their fruits. Furthermore, most scientists and technologists hope that their discoveries will be used to bring good to the world. But due to the workings of Satan, these same technologies become tools—evil tools—in the hands of misguided men and women, malevolent world leaders and, eventually, the Antichrist. High technology is preparing the way for the Beast.

Ample evidence shows that overdependence on science and technology fosters the attitude that God is either unnecessary, unreal, or irrelevant. For example, one writer for a major scientific magazine stated that gene-splicing has put "the whole gene pool of our planet . . . at our disposal," adding that "the key to the living kingdom has been put into our hands." Though such phraseology is perhaps nothing more than hyperbole—words written to make a subject exciting to readers—it does exemplify a certain attitude. This attitude holds that man, not God, is master of creation and that science is at the center of the universe.

As high technology dramatically transforms our lives, people harden their hearts to God and become dependent on technology and science for fleeting happiness and peace. In the next few decades, we will see an incredible explosion in high-tech discoveries and scientific breakthroughs. But with each step toward progress in science, you can be assured that God will recede in the minds of men and women. The tragedy of our era—the end time—is that Satan has convinced the masses that science *proves* that the personal God of the Bible does not exist and is not needed by sophisticated worldly men. The future reality, then, is *more science and less God,* because man's faith in God is, regrettably, diminished in direct proportion to his progress in science and technology.

It is strange that this should be the case, for the all-knowing God is the creator and shaper of nature. Science and technology should be recognized by men as the very essence of God's majesty and the proof of his existence. Many critics of Christianity claim that Christians oppose science, that God's church works to hold back technological progress. But this isn't the case; at least, it isn't true of mainstream Christians. What most Christians oppose is not science, but the perversion of science and the use of technology for evil purposes: war, murder, persecution. Christians are saddened when science is used to demean God and scientists use so-called knowledge to deny God's existence or the power of his works. Historically, Satan has always worked to warp the true meaning of science and use it to divert man's attention from the things of God.

We note, for example, that even in the days of the early church, Satan labored to use science for his own purposes. In 1 Timothy 6:20, Paul encourages Timothy to hold to God's Word in the face of opposition from science: "O Timothy, keep that which is committed to thy trust, avoiding profane and vain babblings, and oppositions of science falsely so called." Here we see Paul's understanding that any science which denies the truth of God is "profane," consists of "vain babblings," and is not empirical, true science at all.

IS AN AGE OF BARBARISM JUST AHEAD?

It is important to note that many of the world's greatest scientists *are* Christians. Even among those who do not believe are a number who fear that science and technological progress will lead to widespread abuse and damage to humanity.

In their recent book *The Dehumanization of Man*,[3] Ashley Montagu and Floyd Matson allude to this misuse of science. They find repellant the sexology of psy-

chologists Masters and Johnson, the celebration of
violence in movies and punk rock lyrics, mass advertis-
ing methods, and television programming. They say
that our technological culture is producing a society of
"cheerful robots," cleverly programmed and controlled
by technicians who are the masters holding political
power.

Many scientists concur with this analysis. In his excellent book *Future Life*,[4] Michel Salomon, a noted
French doctor and science editor, interviewed eighteen
renowned scientists, six of whom were Nobel Prize
winners. Salomon asked each their views of the future
and where science might be taking mankind. Their answers were startling. Said Erwin Chargaff, called the
"Father of Bioengineering":

> I see the beginnings of a new barbarism . . .
> which tomorrow will be called a "new culture."
> . . . Naziism was a primitive, brutal, and absurd
> expression of it. But it was a first draft of the so-
> called scientific or pre-scientific morality that is
> being prepared for us in the radiant future.

Chargaff's frightening conclusion was that the world
is on the edge of catastrophe, brought about by the
abuse of science. "Before every catastrophe," he
warned, "as before an earthquake, there are signs of
what is to come."

The "new culture" that Chargaff warned about is already fast taking shape. And just as Chargaff envisioned, the new barbarism comes cloaked with
respectability, cleverly disguised as the *only* rational religion for twenty-first-century scientific man.

Another Nobel Prize-winning scientist interviewed by Dr. Saloman was Belgium's Christian deDuve. Echoing Chargaff's fears, deDuve solemnly remarked:

> I am convinced that the future is going to find man face to face with some very grave tests— tests that in one way or another will be linked with the abuse of certain kinds of scientific and technical progress. . . . For it *not* to happen, humanity would have to acquire, very rapidly, a heavy dose of wisdom. And today's world would not seem to warrant this happening.

Perhaps the most revealing statement was that of Gabriel Nahaus, world-famous biochemist and researcher:

> I believe that twentieth-century man is intoxicated by all the technological conquests that have been made, in particular the conquest of space and the moon landing.

Intoxication! Is Nahaus correct? Does scientific progress make man drunk with pride and obliterate any and all thoughts of God in his heart? The evidence seems to indicate that it does. Indeed, the evidence tells us that man is beginning to believe in his own omnipotence. Man is coming to believe that *he* is God. This is exactly what Satan wants mankind to believe.

In the following chapters we will look at how man, drunk with pride, has pushed earth to the very brink of destruction. In examining the potential hazards of technological abuse, I am not trying to be an alarmist. A state of panic accomplishes nothing and it is not appropriate for Christians, who ultimately must trust in Almighty God. However, we do need to be aware of how technology is developing and how close we may be to unprecedented worldwide mayhem. If it is foolish to yield to despair and panic, it is also foolish to assume that science and technology will correct its own mistakes and lead mankind to global bliss. Such naivete ignores man's past—and fails to recognize the dangers in the current abuses of science and technology.

TWO
MAN THE CREATOR: ROBOTICS AND BIOENGINEERING

The technologies of bioengineering and robotics are destined to make fantastic changes in our material world. In the science of bioengineering—often called genetic engineering—more than two hundred companies in the United States alone are working to splice genes and invent new life-forms. Meanwhile, robots have already replaced hundreds of thousands of workers on factory assembly lines. The government's Office of Technology Assessment predicts that as many as one-third of all industrial workers may, by the year 2000, find themselves unemployed—victims of robots and automation. In Japan we get a glimpse into the future. There, in the city of Fanue, industrial robots toil seven days a week, twenty-four hours a day, *building new robots.*

Experts in robotics and artificial intelligence are working hard to perfect lifelike robots with silicon chip brains that can think, make independent judgments, and take actions *without* the assistance of humans. By the year 2000 or shortly thereafter, biological engineering—which has already created bacterial life-forms in the lab—will wed its knowledge to that of the roboticists. "Biological chips"—fleshly substances—will be used to construct the brains of robots. Several companies are already working on this project.

In his fascinating book *The Intimate Machine: Close Encounters with Computers and Robots,* [1] Englishman Neil Frude says that soon we shall have robots as companions and even as sex partners. This will be made possible by new achievements in robotics technology looming on the horizon, achievements which include the use of materials similar to human flesh and the manufacture of organic "brains," or biological computer units. This is not science fiction malarkey. It is reality.

Gorham International, a highly regarded technology research and development firm in Gorham, Maine, says that a billion dollar biochip industry is rapidly developing. According to the firm, the biochip will be a stupendous technological advance drawing on "quantum engineering" that will eventually produce the ultimate molecular computer: "The biochip revolution has indeed begun. Scores of technologists in public and private laboratories around the world are joining in a research effort that will occupy the talents of tens of thousands in the 1990s." [2]

Stanley Wellborn, in *U.S. News and World Report* (Dec. 31, 1984), reported on the biochip revolution, which he called "the race to create a living computer":

> Man-made organic computers might be able to detect their own internal design flaws and even

repair and replicate themselves. Miniscule computers implanted in the brain could monitor body chemistry and correct imbalances. They could connect with the human nervous system, serving as artificial eyes, ears, and voice boxes.

In *High Technology* magazine (February 1984), editor Jonathan Tucker stated that a prototype "biochip" may be developed within the next decade, and he reported that a great deal of money has already been spent on biochip research by the U.S. Naval Research Laboratory and the Small Business Administration. And in 1984 in Santa Monica, California, the National Science Foundation, supported by government funding, conducted a conference attended by thirty-five prominent scientists and engineers to explore the potential uses of biochips. At that conference, one UCLA scientist stated: "The National Science Foundation told us this was the most controversial meeting it has ever supported, and one of the most exciting."

Robotics is a science that offers wonderful benefits for mankind. But progress in this field and in bioengineering does have potential for harm due to the perversion of Satan. Arthur C. Clarke, world-famous author of *2001: A Space Odyssey* and numerous other futuristic books, believes that the statement "God made man in his own image" is ticking away like a time bomb at the foundations of Christianity.

Clarke made his remark when asked what would be the effect on civilization if man found extraterrestrial life on other planets. But what of *life created by man* here on earth? The introduction of intelligent robots and manmade biological life in the laboratory is already tearing away at the foundations of Christianity. In the thinking of many people, man is divine, mankind is a creator, and God is therefore either nonexistent, irrelevant, impotent, or at best no more than the equal of man.

THE NEW SPECIES: LIVING MACHINES

In a thorough analysis of what robots will mean to humanity, Geoff Simons of the National Computer Center in Manchester, England, found "there is overwhelming evidence that we are now witnessing the birth of a new family of living species on earth—and this must be seen as one of the momentous events in the history of life."

Simons proposes that the emergence of artificial life is happening in societies—such as America and Great Britain—where religious creeds are in decline.

In his book *Are Computers Alive?* Simons states that a new family of living species "must inevitably tend to strengthen the idea that supernatural components are redundant in any adequate definition of life." In other words, once man has himself created life, then God's creation will be discredited. Frightening, too, is Simons's remark that "perhaps a new generation of theologians will worry endlessly about whether a soul inhabits the silicon chip."[3]

The ultimate goal of a number of distinguished scientists is to develop robots—called self-replicating robots—so intelligent that they can, in turn, independently create other robots. Physicist Robert Freitas, Jr., recently presented to a NASA conference the idea of using these kinds of robots for space exploration. In an article for *Omni* magazine, Freitas said that the robots will reproduce themselves using only sunlight and the earth materials at hand. In other words, the new robot would mimic God's creation by creating life from the dust of the earth. Furthermore, Freitas stated that the creator robot could be built in the next twenty years, remarking that "much of the preparatory work toward this dream has already been done."[4]

George von Tiesenhausen, formerly assistant director of the Advanced Systems Office at the Marshall Space Flight Center in Huntsville, Alabama, and now a vice-president of General Motors, agrees that a robot-creator system can become operational within twenty years. Space authority Robert Frosch, former NASA administrator, was quoted in the *Omni* article as saying that the necessary development "could be accomplished in a decade or so."

Significantly, Frosch, one of America's most respected research scientists and engineers, has said (*Astronautics and Aeronautics,* July/August 1983) that "robotics and artificial intelligence confer on us Hindu godlike extensions of 'self.'" Accordingly, Frosch believes the new hybrid man-machine systems "raise important new questions of engineering ethics."

Scientists Freitas, Frosch, and von Tiesenhausen are honorable men, and I am sure their intention is not to build or promote a robot system that might result in man's alienation from God. Their goal is undoubtedly to better mankind's existence. It is not science we must disparage and criticize, but Satan. Satan takes the worthwhile achievements of science and uses them to diminish God in the eyes of a public that, as Gabriel Nahaus so aptly observed, is intoxicated with technological sophistication.

MAN: THE CREATOR OF ROBOT LIFE

The idea of developing living machines is not new, as I stated in my 1987 book, *Robotica:*

> The notion of a synthetic man, an artificial life form, or an intelligent machine has occupied the fertile imagination of philosophers, writers, and scientists throughout history. Myth has been piled atop myth and concept atop fantasy, all building on the theme of man exercising a measure of divine power by infusing life into inanimate objects or inorganic materials. . . . The invention of robots both in fact and in fiction seems to be the result of a psychological drive, even a behavioral instinct, in *homo sapiens* to be a creator.[5]

In *Robotica* I granted that the economic desire of employers to construct robotic machines to accomplish heavy industrial work and replace men on assembly lines and elsewhere is also a factor in their invention. But I also noted that "for some humans the yearning to manufacture artificial beings involves a quest to control and master destiny, to emulate God or to demonstrate independence of a supreme being."

What man has accomplished so far in designing robot life is nothing short of fantastic. The first electronic computer, ENIAC, developed in 1948, was a monstrosity the size of a barn. Yet it did not have the calculating and mental work power of today's least expensive home computers. Now, less than four decades later, computers that can process millions of bits of data at scorching speed have proliferated throughout the world, and the brain of these computers is so tiny it can fit into one's palm. Some computers' brains (microchips called *central processing units*) are as small as a corn flake. These small brain units fit easily inside a robot's physical structure. Thanks to these powerful new microchip brains, the robot is fast becoming a living being, a "near person."

The development of fifth-generation, thinking computers is a project pursued vigorously by scientists in Japan and the United States. Both nations are also devoting massive resources to the invention of biochips. Professor Toshihiro Akaike of Tokyo University has already unveiled an experimental biochip, made of living flesh, that performs basic microchip computer functions. So we are only a few years away from an even greater brain for machine life. Meanwhile, at Tsukuba University in Japan, Ohio State University, the University of Rhode Island, and dozens of other research centers, engineers are busy perfecting robotic mechanical systems.

In the United States, mega-corporations such as General Electric, Westinghouse, and IBM are spending millions on advanced robotic research. In a 1983 report on the future, AT & T predicted that the turn of the century may well see "teleopresence robots," robots electronically connected with a human's sensory organs. Such a robot could visit a foreign country, and its remote human owner could view the distant scenes and communicate with the people there from long distance.

Hans Moravec of Pittsburgh's Carnegie-Mellon University is one of the world's foremost robotics researchers. He believes that robots will be "human equivalent" in twenty years. "It is clear to me," Moravec says, "that we are on the threshold of a change in the universe comparable to the transition from nonlife to life."

Joseph Deken, distinguished former professor of computer science at the University of Texas at Austin and now program director with the National Science Foundation in Washington, states in his newest book, *Silico Sapiens: The Fundamentals and Future of Robotics,* that robotics is the "ultimate technology." "The unthinking development of these power autonomous systems" cautions Deken, "actually represents humankind's *last* effort before progress makes *homo sapiens* obsolete."[6]

Technologists working in robotic and biotechnology research do not worry, of course, about man someday becoming obsolete. The possibility that artificial life might someday seize power from human overlords is far too distant. What they are concerned about is the potential for commercial applications of new lifeforms. Their immediate aim is to make money; but throughout society, the attitude looms that man is a co-creator with God, or even the *only* creator in a universe without a personal God.

One is reminded of Herman Melville's 1855 tale, "The Bell Tower." In that story, a great but arrogant mechanical genius named Bannadonna creates an amazingly lifelike automaton to strike a great bell in a majestic tower precisely at prescribed times. But on the day the automaton is scheduled to commence its operation, startled officials find Bannadonna, badly mutilated and lifeless, at the foot of the iron automaton. It seems that while the great mechanician was putting his lifelike creation through a test run, he carelessly obstructed the path of the iron figure which, mistaking him for the bell, struck the hapless Bannadonna with its solid hammer.

Author Melville suggests that this was no mere accident; tragedy befell the ambitious Bannadonna because of his inflated human pride in desiring to emulate God and exalt himself as a creator. Concludes Melville, "So the blind slave obeyed its blinder lord; but in obedience slew him. . . . And so pride went before the fall."

HALF MAN, HALF MACHINE: SACRILEGE OR OPPORTUNITY?

Joseph Deken and a number of other thoughtful scientists and engineers are especially concerned about the drive to fuse living creatures and artificial systems: robots made of biological material or human beings with computerized implants—the result of the booming new field called *bionics*.

"There are," Deken warns, "fundamental ethical issues raised by robot-biological symbiosis." He points to the proposal by psychologist B. F. Skinner to implant devices in the brains of livestock to act as electronic lassos. Is such an idea humane, Deken asks, or is it an abuse of technology?

Joseph Weizenbaum, eminent computer science researcher from MIT, also is uneasy about the new developments in bionics, robotics, and other technologies. He cautions that these might be "the penultimate act in the drama separating man from nature." Weizenbaum expresses fears about the future:

> Man's senses are to be read only through pointer readings, flashing lights and buzzing sounds

produced by instruments attached to him as speedometers are attached to automobiles. The ultimate act of the drama is, of course, the final holocaust that wipes out life altogether.[7]

Weizenbaum is most alarmed about research underway to couple an animal's visual system and brain to computers. He contends that this "represents an attack on life itself."

However, mainstream scientists are not about to refrain from pressing forward in robotics, computer, and bionics research, no matter how scary the implications. At New York University Medical Center, neuroscientists Rudolfo Llamas and Kerry Walton have surgically removed the brains of dozens of guinea pigs and kept them in isolation for up to ten hours in their lab. Their stated purpose: to study the relationship between different parts of the brain, making future research on the human brain possible. Other researchers are attempting brain grafts.

Scientists hope to find out not only how the human brain works but how they can improve its function. Some believe they will soon be able to insert a biochip inside a human brain which might, say, contain advanced encyclopedic knowledge or have preprogrammed instructions that direct the body to ward off disease, lose fat, or retain memory. They envision the day when man's intelligence will be amplified to superhuman status by the fusion of computers and biological material and its merger with the human brain.

G. Harry Stine, an author and technologist widely respected in scientific circles, has said that in only a few more years the first tiny microchip computers will be implanted in the human brain. Progress then will come quickly, Stine believes, culminating in an advanced human-machine system.

Stine favors such a system, maintaining that when combined with new discoveries in how the brain functions and processes thought, the new hybrid system will enable man to assume mental powers equivalent to those now exercised by Eastern yogis, shamans, and other "holy men": "The most advanced techniques of yoga and other mental disciplines will be recorded and analyzed using intelligence amplifiers, and computer software will be available that will permit you to achieve whatever level of meditative condition you wish."[8]

A STEP TOWARD GODHOOD FOR MAN?

The technology of life creation is a potential boon for scientists and laymen who suggest it can help usher in the grand millennium during which man will finally ascend to godhood. The combination human-robot creature and the use of machines to expand man's consciousness are welcomed with open arms by many secular thinkers. They look with delight on Joseph Deken's conclusion in *Silico Sapiens* that "the intelligence of a robot can guide the construction of entirely new sense channels and probes."

Author and scientist Arthur C. Clarke views favorably the advent of thinking machines, the extension of the human intellect by electronics, and the coupling of minds to computers. In *Profiles of the Future* he foresees a far-off cosmic evolutionary future in which strange, super beings gather all knowledge. Clarke sounds almost ecstatic when he remarks, "They will not be like gods, because no gods imagined by our minds have ever possessed the powers they will command."[9]

Clarke has on a number of occasions denied the existence of the personal, transcendant God described in the Bible. He predicts that true "consciousness expansion" for man—super intelligence—will be achieved by the twenty-first century. Within an additional hundred years, Clarke believes that brain transplants will be successful and also that a "world mind" will come into existence. He confidently predicts that by A.D. 2100 human immortality will be achieved.

In *The Second Genesis: The Coming Control of Life*, Albert Rosenfeld suggests that technology presents a vision of nirvana on earth. With computerized brain supplements and the expected discoveries in biotechnology, he says, "every man can be his own Shakespeare, Michelangelo, Beethoven, and Newton combined. In fact, what formerly passed for creative genius may seem puny compared to the shining, technological raptures to come."[10]

Joseph Deken is not nearly as optimistic as Rosenfeld, Clarke, and other enthusiasts. He discusses laboratory experiments in which rats will ignore food and water while devoting all their attention to manipulating an electronically linked brain implant until they collapse:

> It is impossible to view these experiments without a dread that they foretell a tragic human deflection. A technology of addiction is only the natural complement to our addiction to technology. "Drug" addicts of the next century may

readily prefer electronic devices to chemical ingestion in their flight from reality.[11]

Deken calls man's belief that he can rely on machines for pleasure and contentment one of the greatest traps of human delusion. He sees trouble ahead because people have begun to adopt the idea that such robotic prostheses as brain supplement devices will be humankind's key to expanded physical well-being, scientific perception, and artistic creativity. Deken realizes that the flood tide of technology cannot now, at this late date, be stemmed. He predicts that robots "will ultimately be immortal, a race of individuals who can repair themselves and download their internal essence completely from older mechanisms to new designs."

Deken's prediction may well come true. Frank Tipler, professor at Tulane University in New Orleans, noting the commonly held scientific belief that "intelligent life is ultimately information processing," recently stated, "The first step is to build hybrids of men and computers. The final step is to get rid of people altogether and transfer the real part of the human—the program—entirely into silicon circuits."[12]

THE QUEST FOR IMMORTALITY

Man has always sought to overcome the law of life that ascribes to him only a set number of years in the mortal flesh on this planet. Immortality and indestructability are still the chief preoccupations of the human race. It is therefore understandable that men might see in robots and artificial life-forms the vehicle for achieving their own immortality. It is being seriously proposed that in the future the totality of a man's brain—its entire store of knowledge and sensations—be transferred to a biocomputer. That biocomputer could then be installed into the anatomy of a robot. Presto! Immortality!

Apart from robotic technology, science is coming up with other astonishing discoveries that might point the way toward immortality. Synthetic body parts have become commonplace, ranging from mechanical hearts to bionic substitutes for bones. An artificial ear is restoring the gift of sound to some persons who were once profoundly deaf, while an artificial larynx has miraculously allowed people whose speech faculties were damaged to once again speak. Scientists in Britain have even constructed a bionic nose that can distinguish between dozens of flower smells.

In other medical research, scientists have been able to regenerate damaged skin, and the prospect is that entire body limbs and organs will soon be grown in laboratories from single cells extracted in advance from the recipient's own body. In 1986, researchers at MIT produced living artificial blood vessels, and a research team at Harvard University Medical School announced the successful cloning of a molecule which triggers the growth of body cells. "Generation of organs has been the stuff of scientific dreams for decades," says Professor Bert L. Vallee, head of Harvard's seven-member team of researchers. "It is now a reality."

Biotechnologists have also been successful in another realm: They have now, for the first time, been able to retard aging. At Hebrew University in Jerusalem, researchers manipulated DNA chemicals to change aged mouse cells back into young cells. They found that rejuvenated fourteen-day-old cells began to behave like four-day-old cells. The work done so far is primitive and cannot be directly applied to humans, but it does represent significant progress. Much other biotechnological research is being accomplished on the aging process. We evidently are only a few decades away from astonishing discoveries in this field.

Courtesy of technology, immortality—the fountain of youth—is several decades off at best, if it ever can be achieved, and if God permits it to happen. But the concept is being considered as a viable future possibility. Jesus promises us eternal life if we trust in his Word and invite the Holy Spirit into our lives. Rejecting this promise, we are off on a desperate quest to guarantee eternal security for ourselves.

IS MAN A TRUE CREATOR?

Science has successfully dispelled the notion that man cannot be a creator. He can, indeed, be a creator; but man is not *the* Creator. The great "I Am" of the Bible set the universe in its moorings by the use of intelligence so infinite and so powerful we can scarcely imagine its existence.

Man, the creature who can create, has long sought to create an environment in which slaves would do his bidding. When human slaves fell out of favor, he turned to machines and other technological devices. Now he has begun to produce intelligent robots—actually androids—that take on a human dimension. And he has, through biotechnology, infused life into rudimentary organisms that are designed to perform assigned tasks. Yet, man's technological creation is a derivative of God's original creation. Man is not a deity but a semiskilled craftsman whose creative knowledge is puny compared to the Master Craftsman.

Robotic and bioengineered life *prove* a Supreme Intelligence (God) created man. If intelligent man can now, *without evolution,* create a being with consciousness—a being that exists external to himself—this is persuasive, almost definitive evidence that man himself was created by an external Intelligence. Diehard evolutionists, who claim man evolved over millions of years through natural selection, from inert chemical elements, one-celled creatures, and finally mammals must now admit that evolution is not an immutable law of nature. Humbly, they should attest that creation by a Supreme Creator is not only possible, it is a certainty. If the scientist who now rejects the Book of Genesis as the story of creation was truly objective, he would understand that man's science has affirmed his own divine creation by a more powerful transcendent God.

MAN'S GOD-GIVEN SOUL

Those who equate man-made and God-made life fail to understand the one vital difference between the two: the creation of God possesses a soul that has been invited by God to accept his Holy Spirit. Humans are spiritual in nature. A human is more than a composition of biological parts. Christ emphasized this when he said to Nicodemus:

> Except a man be born of water and of the Spirit, he cannot enter into the kingdom of God. That which is born of the flesh is flesh; and that which is born of the Spirit is spirit. (John 3:5, 6)

The robot and the lab-created life-form are, indeed, scientific marvels, but the theory that man-made life either disproves God's creation or makes it redundant is one of Satan's most disingenuous frauds.

LIFE MADE TO ORDER: REDESIGNING NATURE

It's known as bioengineering, molecular biology, genetic engineering, gene-splicing, cloning, or simply *biotechnology*. These are some of the terms used to describe the science of producing new life-forms and reshaping or improving existing ones. Biotechnologists seek to discover how a cell's genes are constructed. DNA is the substance in the gene whose composition determines the form an organism—including the human body—will take and its physical characteristics such as height, hair and eye color, intelligence, and other features. DNA is the *code,* or blueprint, for life.

Science has discovered that the DNA genetic code is the basis for all plant and animal life. Techniques such as gene-splicing and cloning have been mastered; these enable scientists to design (or redesign) life-forms. This is the essence of genetic, or biological, engineering. New bacteria species have been created, including a sea-based bacterium that literally eats petroleum. This new life-form will soon be used to clean up oil spills. Nutrasweet (aspertame) artificial sweetener is also an example of a bioengineered product. New biotechnologically produced drugs are being designed that offer the hope of curing previously incurable diseases such as cancer and diabetes and preventing mental illness and birth defects.

Biotechnology holds much promise as a boon to

mankind; but, unfortunately, the negative side of this technology contains the seeds of destruction. As science continues its breakthroughs and as additional complex, sophisticated genetic codes are discovered, it becomes possible to produce products and accomplish feats that already are called "godlike." For example, it will be possible to intervene at conception to engineer the developing fetus, creating a predetermined formula baby. Sex and physical traits, perhaps even the levels of intelligence and physical dexterity, will be preselected.

In previous generations, this was called "eugenics" and in its crude state was a terribly abused science. Now it is becoming sophisticated, and its abuse may also become sophisticated—and more malignant. But scientists seem blind to this possibility. A quarter of a century ago, eminent French biologist Jean Rostrand confidently looked forward to a time "when each human infant (in embryo) could receive a standard DNA that would confer the most desirable physical and intellectual statistics." Rostrand foresees an advantage in that "such children will not be the offspring of a particular couple, but of the entire (human) species."[13] Rostrand's desires may soon be realized.

Biotechnologists are painting for us a not-too-distant future in which human life may be configured according to specification. There are no limits scientifically. A human can be engineered with gills so he can maneuver under the seas without need of a source for air; he can be made stronger and more muscular to do heavy work or participate in a sort of twenty-first-century super-Olympics.

Fruits, vegetables, and trees are already being redesigned to meet economic needs: square tomatoes are on the horizon, for instance. Animals can also be designed as the economy dictates. Beef cattle can be made larger or smaller, fish enlarged to twice their usual size (this has already been done), "barkless" dogs produced without vocal cords. Freeman Dyson, a respected astronomer and physicist, has even proposed that within the next quarter of a century, space scientists and biologists will begin work on a gigantic, living spacecraft in the form of a bioengineered caterpillar that metamorphoses in space into an intelligent space butterfly complete with telescopic eyes and antennae for receiving and transmitting radio signals.[14]

Jeremy Rifkin, who in his book *Algeny* sounded the alarm against what he terms the sacrilege of man designing living material to please himself, commented, "The thought of recombining living material into an infinite number of new combinations is so extraordinary that the human imagination is barely able to grasp the transition at hand."

Rifkin recognizes the incredible implications of a science that confers upon man the power to be creator and molder of life. He protests the new philosophy emerging out of this capability:

> Living things are no longer perceived as carrots and peas, foxes and hens, but as bundles of [coded] information. All living things are drained of their aliveness and turned into abstract messages. Life becomes a code to be deciphered. There is no longer any question of sacredness or

inviolability. . . . How can anything be sacred when there are no longer any recognized boundaries to respect?[15]

In 1986 Rifkin and the scientific director of the Humane Society of America went to court accusing the U.S. Agriculture Department of violating "the moral and ethical canons of civilization" by allowing the insertion of human genes into the genes of animals, thus creating different life-forms. Unfortunately theirs is a minority view, and the quest for control of life continues.

(It should be mentioned here that Rifkin is himself a New Ager, though he belongs to the once dominant wing of the New Age movement, the wing that preaches ecology and a "back to the earth" philosophy.)

Increasingly, the growing legions of prosperity-conscious, technology- and entrepreneurial-oriented yuppies have superseded and supplanted people who, like Rifkin, have been reluctant to embrace scientific and technological progress. Those who favor progress now try to show that the newest technological advances could actually provide *greater* protection for the environment. For example, an artificial microbe, sprayed on plants, protects them from frost damage; others make plant crops disease-resistant. Biotechnology research has also successfully produced plants that create their own natural fertilizers, reducing the need for chemical fertilizers. So the claim is being made that technology is the *answer* to ecological concerns.

Furthermore, biotechnology provides a rationale for

the popular idea of an ongoing evolutionary process destined to genetically catapult man into a higher stage of consciousness. (See Appendix II for the New Age view of this.) So while Rifkin's rapidly diminishing faction preaches moderation in adopting new technologies, many scientists and laymen see science and technology as the way to a heaven on earth. This is why author Arthur C. Clarke has said that, "The technologies that could destroy us can also be used for our salvation."

THE BRAVE NEW WORLD OF BIOTECHNOLOGY

The beginnings of a brave new world seem finally to have arrived. Those who oppose the Bible herald biotechnology as the final demonstration of man's omniscience and divinity and the final cutting of his ties to an outmoded God. Rosenfeld (*The Second Genesis: The Coming Control of Life*) trumpets, "When man can write out detailed genetic messages of his own, his powers become truly godlike." James Watson and Francis Crick, the British scientists who were the first to break the genetic code, contended that DNA is not only the depository of all information but the "sole creator." Astronomer, author, and TV personality Carl Sagan, who believes that the cosmos exists and that's all, remarked that "the stuff of life is everywhere. There's nothing magic about that. . . . We are beings who have just recently evolved on a very ancient world."[16]

Many scientists turn to biotechnology as the science that explains the cosmology of the universe. The universe is perceived to be a complex system of unfathomable trillions of energy molecules and subatomic particles, combined into genetically coded *information systems*. Man is seen as an information system which, much like a computer, constantly seeks more information to add to his genetic constitution.

The popular theory of *transformational evolution* should be mentioned here. Applied to biotechnology, this theory asserts that man is an evolving creature whose mission is to expand his consciousness. This is the biocomputer equivalent to expanding one's information base. To possess a higher level of consciousness is to be more intelligent and knowledgeable, to have an awareness, to be awake—in essence, to be a more advanced information system.

Transformational evolutionists profess a belief in the *inevitability* of the human evolutionary process. It is written in the stars that man's destiny is to become a creature with higher consciousness.[17] From this conclusion comes the dangerous assertion, made by Sir Julian Huxley, that man is preprogrammed to be "the sole agent of further evolutionary advance on the planet." According to this concept, man has the awesome and inescapable task of assuming for himself the role of architect of the universe.

The crux of this position is the belief that the most extreme practices of biotechnology are not violations of nature. Instead, bioengineering is a necessary outgrowth of nature's own evolutionary process. Man not only has the right to be a creator; he violates nature if he *fails* to assume this right.

Jeremy Rifkin put his finger on the very pulse of the emerging cosmology and the disturbing new worldview when he ominously warned that "our children will be convinced that their creations are of a far superior nature to those from which they were copied. . . . They will seek to transform the living world into a golden treasure trove, a perfectly engineered, optimally efficient state."

I share Rifkin's fears about the potential for abuse of biotechnology and I agree with his conclusion that, in the new world that is fast taking shape, we will be "responsible to nothing outside ourselves, for we are the kingdom, the power, and the glory for ever and ever."

HOW TO CONSTRUCT THE NEW MAN-GOD

Some New Age scientists and others have proposed that one means of speeding up the evolutionary process toward man's godhood is to fix his genes so that he will arrive into the world ready with an advanced mind endowed with higher consciousness. They hold that we might be able to engineer the infant to genetically yearn for peace, for justice, for sharing. Dr. Konrad Lorenz, Austrian founder of ethology, the study of animal behavior, has put forth the psychological theory that hereditary aggressive drives, or instincts, make man go to war. Many scientists contend that this instinct resides in man's genes. Change the innate gene and, theoretically, you create a sensitive, peace-loving individual.

Many social designers and philosophers believe that biotechnology can be successfully used to recognize and weed out from man's brain the bad genes that cause his awful behavior. What a wonderful world this would be, they exclaim, if all babies were genetically engineered with all the best traits. Edward Cornish, editor of *The Futurist* magazine and president of the World Future Society, professes a belief in what is being called *positive genetic engineering:*

> Human nature developed over millions of years when man existed in a savage or barbaric state. Now that we live in a technological civilization, perhaps we should bring about such modifications as reducing the sex drive, or making people less aggressive, less lustful, less selfish. We could make ourselves into saints capable of creating a heaven on earth.[18]

In his acclaimed book *The Selfish Gene*, biologist Richard Dawkins suggested ways to bring about gentle and generous people. He contended we might deliberately cultivate and nurture pure, disinterested altruism. Dawkins admits that man in his current state is often evil and selfish. But, he says, we can change ourselves: "We are built as gene machines . . . but we have the power to turn against our creators. We, alone on earth, can rebel against the tyranny of the selfish replicators."[19]

To Dawkins and others, bad genes—not human sin and not Satan—are the enemies. Genes are the creators, not God. And the only obstacles in the way of a heaven on earth are bad genes. One shudders to think what a future Antichrist might be able to accomplish in a society in which he and his agents are able to select the most desirable genes. The age of the innately cruel

policeman or soldier and the docile citizen may dawn
in man's gloomy tomorrow.

ONLY GOD CAN BUILD THE PERFECT HUMAN

Christians who know their Bible reject the assertions of
those who wish to use biotechnology as a tool to drive
a wedge between man and God. But we cannot hope to
reverse the scientific knowledge that biotechnology
represents, nor is that action necessary. We should understand that neither biotechnology nor any other science is inherently bad. We cannot allow ourselves to be
unfairly branded as antiscience and antiprogress. But
we must oppose the idea that science itself refutes the
truths of Christianity. God wants us to support a scientific attitude that exalts him, a science that honors his
kingdom.

When reasonable men look at the complexities of
the information systems that comprise the trillions of
living organisms on our planet at this instant, they
stand in awe of the Great Intelligence who created this
monumental collection. Man's computers whir and
cogitate in an often vain attempt to decipher codes that
are the blueprints for life. But isn't it phenomenal that
we who are children of the Most High God and who
love and are loved by him can, through prayer, talk to
the One who instantaneously commanded all these
complex codes into existence? We have a direct line to
the keeper of the blueprints!

Only the keeper of the blueprints can transform man
into a loving, righteous creature who yearns for peace
and who practices brotherhood. Man's mind alone

can't perform this miraculous transformation, nor will science ever produce the "perfect human" designed in a laboratory. The Holy Spirit is the aspect of God that works to create the new man.

During the two millennia after the first coming of Christ man has learned so much yet remains so unwise. Seeking to exalt himself as a god, man has become less than a man. Now he perceives himself as an information system, a mere machine to be reconfigured and tinkered with much as a youngster builds and rebuilds a hot rod. Man builds slave robots to serve him, unaware that he may himself become enslaved as their intelligence grows to exceed his. He devises techniques to engineer behavior directly into human fetuses, unthinkingly bequeathing to a future dictator or even a tyrannical majority the power to alter and limit his consciousness. Yet he does so in the hope that his consciousness will be expanded. The psalmist implored God, "What is man, that thou art mindful of him?" But the science of these, the last days, arrogantly asks, "What is God, that man is mindful of *him?*"

THREE
A GLOBAL BRAIN FOR MANKIND: COMPUTERS

Like robotics and biotechnology, the computer may also be used for good or evil. The computer is a major factor in our society and has radically altered almost every aspect of industry and every feature of our daily lives. But its emergence has given some an excuse for degrading God and his creation.

Norbert Weiner, one of the founders of the computer science of *cybernetics,* called it "the science of communication and control in the animal and machine." Although recognized as one of the great thinkers in the field of computers, Weiner believed that the danger of overdependence on computers ranked with that of nuclear destruction and overpopulation.

Thus we see that the computer is an instrument of control. With it we can control and manipulate massive amounts of information. But, as computer scientist Jacques Vallee noted in his remarkable book *Network Revolution,* "There is no such thing as obtaining information without obtaining a measure of control over

. . . persons."[1] The dangers in control by computer, warns Vallee, are clear.

Vallee also commented on the tremendous growth in popularity of smaller personal, home, and office microcomputers. According to Vallee, prominent scientists such as Dr. Michael Grab have suggested the building of a "global brain for mankind"—a gigantic supercomputer into which all other distant computers can be linked. But, asks Vallee, "Is it desirable to build it?"

To him the answer may well be no, for he detects the growth of a computer world out of control, a world where data and numbers have taken the place of values, where reality is digitally dissolved and truth may be unrecognizable. "I have concluded from my work with computers," he cautions, "that we are no longer in control of this exploding technology. But we can still hope to influence the general direction of the beast."

Note Vallee's description of computer technology as "the beast." It is perhaps a fitting choice of words, because in the years to come, high technology growth will occur in lockstep pace with other end-time events. The Antichrist who is to come—the Beast with the number 666—will have, in computers and other technologies, ready-made tools with which to control populations and punish those who defy his malignant reign.

The stated goal of some computerists is to create a "wired world" where everyone, every home, and every office is connected by a video screen and computer terminal. All reading and learning and most work would be accomplished by computer networking. However, Vallee noted in his book that computer networks can be used by a repressive government to look for undesirables or to pinpoint suspects. This fact has caused a government commission in Sweden to comment in an official report about the growing use of networking and video technology: "Computer technology can always be silently used to check who learns what." Further, the report warned that immense power accumulates among those who decide what shall be put into such a system and what shall be left out.

Many other authorities are also sounding the alarm about the dangers of unrestricted computer abuse. *New York Times* correspondent David Burnham recently wrote *The Rise of the Computer State,* which reveals in great detail how computer technology can be used to threaten the privacy of the individual and to gain political power. According to Burnham, computerized records of credit card companies, insurance and telephone companies, hospitals, hotels, churches, and airlines can be obtained and exploited through a worldwide telecommunications network of linked data bases. All that's necessary for ultimate abuse, says Burnham, is for a government to have the will to use the systems for evil purposes.[2] In the last days, the Bible proclaims, Satan will provide that will.

MAN AS COMPUTER, COMPUTER AS GOD

During my military career and, more recently, as an author of technology-oriented books and head of my own consulting firm, I have been acquainted with the newest technologies in fields ranging from lasers to robotics and high-tech military weaponry. I have always viewed computers and other technologies as nothing more than tools. To me, God is supreme over man and man over his tools, or at least that's the way the world *should* work. But, increasingly, the tendency is for man to conceive of his technological tools as a means to self-empowerment and even exalting himself as a god.

In the long epoch of humanity before computers, man was reluctant to picture himself as a powerful being equal to God. In Darwin's conception of evolution, man was thought to be relatively weak, simply a random, freak creation of nature. However, progress in science and technology and especially in computers has enabled man to paint a new picture of his place in the universe. Darwin's evolutionary theory of random selection is now largely discredited and has been replaced by that of *transformational evolution*. This new theory, discussed in the previous chapter, holds man up as a godlike being capable of transforming the universe and creating his own reality. Transformational evolution places man *in control of evolution*.

Since the theory of transformational evolution is a dramatic departure from previously accepted scientific truth, its advocates have labored mightily to develop a body of additional "truths" to support their idea that divine man is in control. One such "truth" is the suggestion that the universe is a huge computer and that man is also a computer capable of connecting (networking) with the universal computer. In effect, this theory proposes that there is no transcendent God as he is described in the Old and New Testaments. The universal computer system is God; man, as a linking, integral component computer, is also God.

Computer scientist David Foster, an authority on cy-

bernetics, has best stated the new concept in his book
The Intelligent Universe: A Cybernetic Philosophy:

> I put forward a new theory of the universe which
> suggested that the universe was something like a
> gigantic electric computer and that the energeti-
> cal and material interactions could be regarded as
> a sort of cosmic data processing. . . . Since man
> is a part of the intelligent universe then it would
> be reasonable to suppose that he incorporates cy-
> bernetic (computer system) design principles;
> and indeed, a cursory examination of the struc-
> ture of the human psyche and body indicate a
> system basically capable of achieving steersman-
> ship (*cybernetics* comes from the Greek word *ky-
> bernetes,* meaning "steersman").[3]

Foster further proposes that man, the computer,
though he is only a component of the greater universal
computer, can somehow exercise his will to rise up and
become the controller and master of this more powerful
computer. All that is necessary, he contends, is for man
to learn how to program the universal computer. Perhaps this idea is why Timothy Leary, drug guru of the
1960s, now has taken on a new project: He has formed
a computer software company to promote the powers
of the mind. The name for his new company:
"Headware."

PROGRAMMING GOD, THE UNIVERSAL COMPUTER

In essence, Foster and many new thought, New Age
scientists envision the universe as a great computer and

man as the power that tells it what to do. Man makes "God" his obedient servant by programming him to follow commands. Man supposedly rules God with the power of his mind, which is a type of cosmic computer keyboard.

Faith becomes an irrelevant concept because there is no need for it. Faith involves the acceptance of things unseen, but the new scientific theory pretends to have uncovered all that is hidden. There is no supernatural spirit (God) in whom we can place our faith. Man the cosmic computer operator, himself a data information system, merely employs mind power to manipulate a natural process.

To those who view the universe as a massive information processing computer and man as the computer's programmer and operator, a computer program becomes God's Word. In an obvious distortion and abuse of biblical principles, David Foster states that:

> Some of the dogmas of religion may well be true and especially as to "In the beginning was the *Word*" and "Let there be *Light*." For *light* is the mechanics of information and the *Word* is the utter foundation of computer technology.[4]

Contrary to what Christians know to be true, this distorted theory alleges that man can take control over both the *Word* and the *Light*. The transformational evolutionary process shall end in cosmic consciousness, with man crowned and sitting on the universal throne. This is forecasted to occur naturally, as the expanding human mind seeks and acquires more and more information and thereby evolves into a higher-consciousness being with infinite programming power.

If you read the previous chapter of this book, you undoubtedly have observed that some computer scientists and biotechnologists employ the concept of the universe as a system of coded information. Many theorize that man can successfully manipulate this store of coded information to transform and shape the world to his liking. The destiny of the universe, they claim, is solely in man's own hands.

HYPERINTELLIGENCE: THE NEXT EVOLUTIONARY STEP?

Some theorists have recently fabricated another "truth" to support their belief in the deity of man. That truth involves the development and use of computer networks to create a super, or hyper, intelligence. There are now millions of computers in the world, and, increasingly, these legions of computers are being linked through telecommunications. What we can look forward to in the future are global networks of computers. A few such networks already exist; but by the twenty-first century, millions of interconnecting computer systems will crisscross the globe.

Now come the enthusiasts to explain the significance of this technological advancement. In *The Futurist* magazine (December 1984) Dr. George Bugliarello, president of the Polytechnic Institute of New York, says:

> Global networks offer us the possibility of expanding our biological intelligence—an intelligence operating on a global scale and repre-

senting a major evolutionary step for our society and our species.

Bugliarello's view is one shared by many others, including a number of computer scientists. According to this view, evolutionary development started within our own bodies after we had evolved from the lower species. But now, this evolutionary process is being carried out at an accelerated pace by a combination of biological, psychological, and technological factors. The computer is one such factor; indeed, the computer is thought to be the catalyst which will make the next evolutionary step possible.

As global computer networks grow, some people are proposing that all the world's scientific knowledge can be made available to networkers. They foresee global intelligence rapidly evolving. Called *hyperintelligence,* this new state of evolutionary synthesis will, so the theory goes, make possible a revolutionary transformation of society and propel mankind to ever higher levels of achievement. Bugliarello believes that this could ultimately lead to a world language offering access to worldwide computer networks and data banks.

(Though Bugliarello perhaps has not thought of it, his idea of a world computer language reminds us of the attempt by ancient man to build the Tower of Babel, and of God's action to thwart that attempt by causing its builders to speak a multitude of confusing languages.)

A NEW MORALITY

According to Bugliarello, the development of hyperintelligence—spurred by a massive world network of interlinking computers—should lead first of all to a new morality. Bugliarello says that this new morality will result "because by definition it will put us in a broader context, more connected to each other across national and ideological environments." This new morality, he contends, might finally solve such problems as the specter of nuclear and local war and man's inability to develop a decent standard of living for all humanity. Bugliarello asserts that "hyperintelligence, and the global computer networks that make it possible, is the best hope we have to create this new society—to *create* our future rather than just to accept it."

Though Bugliarello speaks of computer hyperintelligence as the "best hope" we have to create a new, better society, God's Word, the Bible, specifically states that Jesus Christ is the *only* hope mankind has to create a new, more perfect society. Many scientists and New Age theorists would have us believe that technology and transformational evolution will be our salvation, but we need only look to the world around us to see that this isn't so. For example, accompanying the spread of computers is a plague of computer crime ranging from financial embezzlement and fraud to unlawful destruction of records. Child sex abusers are known to use computer networks to advertise. Computers are also potentially harmful tools for abuse by spy and law enforcement agencies and totalitarian governments.

As I mentioned earlier, a number of computer specialists have sounded the alarm about the dangers in deifying computers. This danger was perhaps best expressed by H. Dominic Corvey and Neil H. McAlister in their book *Computer Consciousness*: "If we fail to fear the computer's ability to become a latter-day Baal who demands our sacrifices on the altar of technology, then we may, unresistingly, become first its worshippers, and finally its sacrifices."[5]

WHO CREATED THE UNIVERSAL COMPUTER?

Is the universe only a great, gigantic computer with man, the magical computer keyboard operator, destined to become its ultimate master? I consider it nothing less than blasphemy to equate God with a computer to be programmed by man. And if the universe is a sort of computer system, who built it? Who has programmed it to the present day? Who has maintained it and provided it energy? Who has the innate power to relegate it to the trash heap and build for himself a better computer—one that operates more efficiently and more satisfactorily? The answer can only be God, and there's no way we're going to order him around.

The Christian who truly understands science need not subscribe to the perverse computer and biotechnology theory that props up man as an evolving god. In his insightful *The Creation of Life,* A. E. Wilder Smith remarks, "There is no longer any need for the Christian or the believer in God to hide, intellectually speaking, in the catacombs. Today, true science supports the man who believes in a supermaterialistic view of life, the universe, and its future."[6]

Clashing with those who abuse technology to deny God, Wilder Smith points to the vast unlikelihood that the mind-boggling immensity of the universe's store of coded information could have spontaneously sprung into existence from nothingness. "The source of this coding power . . . must be so superior to any intellectual power that we, mortals, have experience of, that for us it can only appear to be infinite."

Three centuries ago the brilliant French scientist-philosopher Blaise Pascal, a Christian, made the statement, "Things which are incomprehensible do not cease to exist." He believed, as all Christians must, that the universe has phenomena which cannot be comprehended by scientific investigation. God is, ultimately, incomprehensible, for he is infinite. But as Pascal observed, our inability to analyze him and encode him into computer data does not mean that he does not exist. Arrogant scientific man has become so obsessed with merely possessing and processing information that he has come to ignore whatever cannot be stored in a computer. A personal God, since he cannot be fully grasped, is simply ignored. God, if referred to at all, is defined as some kind of cosmic information system that can be stored in a computer. But this infinite Intelligence, this Supreme Designer, continues to exist regardless of proud man's desire to deny his presence.

FOUR
STATES OF CHEMICAL BLISS: MIND–ALTERING DRUGS

Robotics, bioengineering, and computers are not the only high technologies that offer both promise and danger. Scientists are on the brink of remarkable discoveries in pharmaceuticals. In a special issue of *U.S. News & World Report* (May 9, 1983), the editors gave readers an exciting glimpse of "what the next fifty years will bring." In discussing drug research, the magazine said:

> The next two decades will usher in a revolution in drug treatments as scientists unlock mysteries of the brain and find effective therapies for such ancient plagues as depression, acute pain, schizophrenia, senility, and perhaps even criminal behavior.

Drug miracles are coming fast and furiously. Experts say that about 75 percent of all drugs ever invented have come on the scene in the last decade. While many will bring victory over cancer, diabetes, and other diseases, some drugs that work on the mind will be controversial because of the potential for their abuse. We are already seeing some magazines and other publications touting the world of tomorrow as a place where man might enjoy "states of chemical bliss."

In researching a book on jobs in high technology fields, I talked with a number of experts in the pharmaceutical field. They described the workings of many of these future drugs, some of which are now being tested. Many are based on advances in biological engineering. I was told drugs will soon be able to:

- Control aggressiveness
- Control fear
- Relieve guilt feelings
- Create pleasant dreams
- Stimulate intelligence
- Control sociability
- Increase memory
- Enhance sexual response
- Induce abortion
- Eliminate venereal diseases
- Cure anxiety
- Prevent obesity

Brain researchers and pharmaceutical makers have worked diligently to map out the chemistry of the brain in great detail. They have already determined the many methods brain cells use to process natural chemicals and hormones. Biotechnologists and chemists believe they will be able to duplicate these chemical and hormonal messengers synthetically. In addition, biotechnology is providing a harvest of new drug compounds that work on the brain to produce various states of consciousness.

Science magazine (November 1985) recently reported on the startling research breakthroughs in brain biochemistry:

> Armed with a flood of newly discovered chemicals and the [biotechnology] techniques of cellular and molecular biology, brain scientists are beginning to track the origins of some of our most basic emotions, drives, and behaviors from the level of genes and molecules to specific nerve circuits and brain systems. What they're finding are the biological underpinnings not only of thirst but also of hunger, pleasure, pain, sexual arousal, and even learning.

Unfortunately, some of the new drugs made possible by brain biochemistry research are capable of doing things to human minds that can only be categorized as hideous in nature. Some can produce nightmares and hallucinations, others docility and apathy, while still others induce such negative emotions as fright, anger, sadness, anxiety, paranoia, and confusion.

Such drugs often turn up as an unexpected consequence of normal pharmaceutical research. (An example is depa provera, a drug that reduces the sex drive in males and has been given to sex offenders convicted of rape and other sex crimes.) Obviously, it is not the intention of pharmaceutical companies to make these available to the public nor even generally to produce them at all. But they exist. Governments want to use such drugs to augment their military's chemical and biological capability or as chemical substances potentially valuable in spy and intelligence work. Later, in discussing new military weapons, we'll see how the Soviet Union devotes many resources to developing new chemical and biological agents for future warfare.

DRUGS OF WONDER AND AWE

Today, miracle drugs are designed to serve the needs of mankind. But think of the awesome horrors that might someday befall mankind as a result of the administering of such drugs. "Malcontents"—those who oppose government authority—could be drugged to control their aggressiveness and render them docile, helpless, and susceptible to propaganda. It is not farfetched to conceive that entire groups or populations may secretly be fed drugs in their food or water supply, drugs that create fear, hallucinations, or sickness. Favored disciples may be given drugs to stimulate intelligence, aid memory, and increase sexual satisfaction, while others less favored would be denied these drugs. Abortion— the killing of the unborn—could become more palatable to the masses because drugs would be used instead of surgical procedures.

Drugs offer certain advantages to totalitarian dictatorships. In his thought-provoking book *What Sort of People Should There Be?* Britain's Jonathan Glover discusses the potential for abuse of mind drugs by evil governments.

> Conditioning techniques, certain drugs, and perhaps some kinds of brain stimulation all alter behavior by altering desire. . . . From the point of

view of governments, rule by fear and torture must be a messy affair, generating problems of its own. It would be much simpler if techniques existed to make people *want* to behave in the desired way.[1]

For those who doubt that drugs would ever be used for such awful purposes, one can only suggest that the example of the Soviet Union be studied. There, dissidents—persons opposed to the Communist regime—are forcibly given injections of horrible drugs which wrack the victim's body for days. Some have been given injections of psychotropic drugs which induce schizophrenia, paranoia, or even lifelong stupor and paralysis. Then, the hospital announces the victim needs long-term psychiatric care or confinement in a government asylum.

In a letter smuggled out of one of the USSR's psychiatric hospital prisons, a Soviet dissident poet, V. I. Chernyshov, told of the horrors inflicted on Soviet Christians being "treated" for mental illnesses in his ward. Begging Christians around the world to help their brothers in suffering, Chernyshov said of himself: "I'm . . . terribly afraid of torture. But there is a worse torture . . . the introduction of chemicals into my mind. . . . I have already been informed of the decision for my 'treatment.' Farewell!"[2]

A DRUGGED SOCIETY

It is easy to view late twentieth-century Western culture as a "drugged society." In the U.S. alone, the Food and Drug Administration estimates that some 10 to 15 billion tranquilizers, stimulants, and other mind-altering and mood-changing drugs are legally manufactured each year. Illegitimate drugs are rampant, with heroin and cocaine addiction at all-time highs. Recently, "designer drugs" have been the social rage. Home basement chemists are finding new ways to synthesize and reformulate compounds to give users new highs. Sadly, many designer drugs turn out to be poisonous and provide unsuspecting recipients the ultimate high: physical death.

A drugged society cannot be a loving, sympathetic society because the effects of drugs are so unreliable and variable. The same drug that produces relaxation in one person may produce apathy and an uncaring attitude in another. Also, considering the extent to which modern society depends on the minds of specialists—airline pilots, computer programmers, medical surgeons, and others—operating at peak peformance, the notion of mind-altering drugs being freely consumed is particularly frightening.

For society as a whole, perhaps the most terrifying and destructive of future drugs will be those that will relieve a person's guilt feelings. Dr. Konrad Lorenz, one of the world's leading psychological researchers, has said that such a drug would be insane. It would, he said, result in "the disappearance of the last safeguards that protect some of us from sadism and homicidal tendencies." It is also easy to see that this drug will free persons under conviction by God for sin and wrongdoing. In the dark days to come, people will no longer be held back by conscience and conviction. Drugs will blot out the last vestiges of morality and restraint. The pangs of conscience will be felt no more.

ACHIEVING GODHOOD THROUGH DRUGS

Even more frightening is the promotion of illegal drug use by some groups as a means of altering one's consciousness. The use of psychedelic drugs, especially LSD, is highly recommended by those who believe that through these drugs the individual can get in touch with his inner self, connect with the Universal Mind, and communicate with spirit guides. Drug highs are thought to be ideal for beginners and initiates who seek to "begin their journey to self-awareness, creativity, mind power, and godhood."

In *The Aquarian Conspiracy,* New Age author Marilyn Ferguson cautiously extols the virtues of psychedelic drugs. She suggests that more advanced students can achieve the same results, after training, through meditation and other psychotechnologies; but she hastens to add, "It is impossible to overestimate the historic role of psychedelics as an entry point."[3]

Ferguson notes that during the 1960s, illegal drugs played a pivotal role in acquainting record numbers of persons with the transformative religious qualities of New Age thinking:

> For tens of thousands of left-brained engineers, chemists, psychologists, and medical students who never before understood their more spontaneous, imaginative right-brained brethren, the drugs were a pass to Xanadu, especially in the 1960s. As one chronicler of the 60s remarked, "LSD gave a whole generation a religious experience."[4]

According to the accounts documented by Ferguson and other writers, many people believe psychedelic drugs help them to achieve unity with "God"—the universe. Ferguson quotes one drug experimenter as saying, "I learned from LSD about alternative realities—and suddenly *all* bibles made sense."[5]

The side effects and dangers of illegal mind-altering drugs give many experimenters pause. While some continue to praise the virtues of psychedelic substances, others have turned to psychotechnology as a safer passage to god status. However, if new, safer mind-altering drugs are discovered, and if governments can be persuaded to abolish laws prohibiting their free use, future generations are increasingly likely to turn to such substances, viewing drug ingestion as a "quick ticket to paradise." A future society—only a few decades away at most—can realistically be conceived in which only the "weirdos"—Christian evangelicals and fundamentalists and others—would refuse to take legally sanctioned, psychedelic mind drugs.

CAN DRUGS HEAL OUR MEMORIES?

Persons suffering from depression often turn to psychotropic drugs for relief. There are prescription drugs—antidepressants and mood-changers—that do offer beneficial relief from attacks of depression. Especially helped are acute manic-depressives, individuals who are inexplicably inflicted with deep, dark moods. There is no doubt that such drugs are needed and should be made available by physicians when medical circumstances dictate.

However, the abuse of antidepressants or any other drug that alters mood and consciousness can prove extremely damaging to one's psychological well-being. Chemicals—whether they be antidepressants, tranquilizers, or alcohol—can be harmful if used to erase or blot from the memory life's disappointments and mental pains and the recollection of negative experiences. No chemical should be used simply to help one "forget."

A number of psychologists and psychiatrists are using drugs and shock therapy, as well as questionable psychotechnologies such as visualization and meditation, to help sufferers erase from their consciousness the thoughts in their conscious or subconscious that currently plague them. By erasing these thoughts, it is believed that "healing of the memories" will occur. Healing of the memories is even advocated by a few Christian psychologists and counselors.

The danger in a "healing of the memories" is that the human brain is not some type of computer with memories to be erased at will and replaced only with positive information, starting over clean. Certainly we desire that memories of such tragic events as a death of a loved one, a tragic and painful divorce, or a bad deed we feel guilty for be committed to the past. Paul said, "I die daily," indicating that though each of us faces difficulties, every day is a fresh start, another opportunity to recommit our lives to Christ and to forge a better life for ourselves and our loved ones. For the Christian, each day should be a fresh miracle.

However, the artificially induced healing of memories is a deception. God does not wish for us to totally erase from our memories all that we've experienced. Surely it is far better to remember and learn from our mistakes, to stay awake and know that each day—like yesterday and the day before—we are able to renew our spirits and pledge to do good. Of course, we must guard against an overwhelming guilt that renders us unable to cope. In fact, Jesus died for us on the cross as a redemption for our sins; he took up for us the burden of guilt.

The point is, God does not want us to have a lobotomy—literally or figuratively; he wants strength, maturity, and character to develop through the example of learning, perseverance, and overcoming. To see the beauty and greatness of flowers that grace a countryside is not to deny that also amidst the flowers might be weeds, chinch bugs, and a bundle of other negatives. The wise lover of nature dwells on the beauty—on the good—but is eager to identify and overcome the bad.

For example, we rightly perceive that death, war, sickness, lies, and deceit are bad things—things we justly would like to alter or erase from reality. Still, they continue to exist because Satan and the evil of this world are real, and only God can create a new reality. With the aid of drugs, hypnosis, visualization, and other mind-absorbers, we might indeed begin to *perceive* the world differently. In this case our minds change, but the world remains the same. Some misguided persons have depended on these substances so much that they withdraw from reality altogether, in effect committing mental suicide.

Some persons want to convince you that through the powers of the mind and through drugs you can create your own reality; but ultimately you can do no more than have confidence in yourself as a person, work to effect positive changes in the world around you, and ask God's help in changing those negative realities that you cannot yourself alter. Each of us can work for positive change, but we can't think it into existence. And the use of drugs to permanently alter reality or to heal memories is a dangerous alternative that renders the user little more than the victim of chemical lobotomy.

FIVE
TECH TOOLS FOR THE ANTICHRIST: THE IRON CLAW OF THE BEAST

There are many references in the New Testament to the rise of an Antichrist, an incarnation of Satan in human form, in the last days just before the second coming of Jesus. Also called the Beast with the number 666, the Antichrist is described in Revelation 13 as a being who will exercise great world power—so great that he will reign "over all kindreds and tongues and nations." The Antichrist will perform wonders and deceive the masses by the means of these miracles. Bible prophecy tells us that, once in power, the Antichrist will usher in the tribulation period, a savage time of dictatorial rule in which Christian believers will suffer intense persecution.

If, as the signs indicate, this is the historical era in which the Antichrist will be elevated to an earthly throne by supernatural forces, it seems clear that he will find in his pantry of terror a vast arsenal of technological tools and devices. In this chapter, we'll take a look at some of these tech tools, but let me first issue a warning: This is not a pleasant subject. It is not fashionable today to dwell on the potential negatives of technology—on the specter of technology gone mad in a Dark Age. But evil exists in this world, and it will not go away simply because we choose not to discuss it.

IS "BIG BROTHER" HERE?

In George Orwell's chilling novel *1984,* much of the world is in the grip of a leader called "Big Brother." Strikingly similar to the Antichrist, this evil leader demands people's total obedience, and he uses every available technological means to control and brutalize the population. In a special issue (January 2, 1984) of *U.S. News & World Report,* the world depicted in George Orwell's famous novel was compared with today's world of high technology. The magazine reported that frightening new tools are increasingly being made available—tools that a future Big Brother might easily choose to use on a tortured society. Examples of these tools include:

- Tiny radio transmitters with microphones the size of a matchhead (available now by mail order for as little as twenty-five dollars).
- Laser beams that can monitor voices through office windows by detecting vibrations from a glass pane.
- Electronic bracelets affixed to the wrists of persons under surveillance. Police are alerted whenever the person leaves his residence without permission. These are now in use in

New Mexico to control and monitor the movement of prisoners on restricted parole.

- Cameras on U.S. Air Force spy satellites miles above Earth can now photograph something as small as the license plate number of an auto or the shape of a man's beard and instantly transmit the picture to a remote screen display.
- Miniature radio transmitters, implantable in humans, that can be activated and traced by skyborne satellites.
- Two-way, interactive cable TV systems backed up by high-speed computers are now in use in a few communities and may be in general use within a decade. Newer, flat-screen TVs that can be hung on the wall will improve the usefulness of such systems.

Technological advances continue to add new and improved devices to the inventory already available to security and police forces and others responsible for clandestine surveillance. Some are developed for benign reasons. An example is a supersensitive sound detection system recently developed by the U.S. Department of Agriculture to detect the presence of fruit-infesting bugs. The sound system is so sensitive it can detect chewing sounds made by a single day-old insect in a grapefruit. Though the intent of such a system is praiseworthy, it could be of great value in the hands of would-be eavesdroppers listening in on citizens from a remote location.

Devices developed originally for valid military use

could be used for foul purposes. One example is night vision devices. American fighting forces were the first to make use of intensified night vision technology in the 1960s. Special scopes, goggles, and other hand-held devices enabled the users to spot enemy forces in near total darkness. Today, that same technology is being adapted in nonmilitary applications. Game wardens in Africa, for example, are using night vision devices to spot poachers who illegally hunt big game under cover of darkness. The devices are also being used by law enforcement agencies, by naturalists studying animal behavior, and by pilots and others who must see in the dark. The Los Angeles Fire Department, for example, fights brush fires at night with helicopters flown by pilots wearing night vision goggles. Night vision devices are also in use by private investigators to spy on citizens on the darkest of nights.

COMPUTER TECHNOLOGIES

Computer technologies have particularly amplified the potential for abuse. For example, a new computer chip so tiny it can barely be seen can be placed under a person's skin with a syringe to serve as a permanent electronic coding or message system. When the chip passes through a magnetic monitoring device, it is read. Manufactured by a California company, these computer chips are currently used to assign high-tech "brands" on cattle and prevent rustling. In the future, say computer experts, they may replace credit cards and other I.D. documents. The chips could be used to identify persons making purchases and to automatically credit or debit their accounts at a financial institution.

The firm making these identification chips is one of

several companies coming out with similar systems. For example, Japan's giant Toshiba Corporation has developed a new "smart" identification card. The new card can electronically transfer funds to stores and from banks, hold a person's entire medical—or criminal— history, and serve as a passport, a social security card, or even register a person's arrival and departure times at airport terminals. Now the size of a regular credit card, future technological advances will allow the card to shrink to a size which allows permanent implantation of the operating chip under the skin of the human body.

Huge computer data banks are constantly getting bigger. The IRS, the FBI, the CIA, and a number of private firms now have access to hundreds of millions of computer dossiers. In late 1985, the super-secret National Security Agency (NSA) opened a highly classified Supercomputer Research Center in Maryland employing one hundred of the United States' top computer experts. According to NSA's director, Lt. Gen. Lincoln Faures, the center, costing an estimated $180 million, will provide "state-of-the-art technological sophistication crucial to the security interests and economic well-being of the United States." This is a laudable goal. Yet, Senator William Cohen of Maine, in a recent committee hearing on computer abuses, warned, "I think we're rapidly approaching a society in which the human voice is not going to be heard above the whir of the computer."[1]

SUPER COPS

In the October 1985 issue of *The Futurist* magazine, Dr. James R. Metts, a law enforcement expert from

Lexington, South Carolina, described the many tech tools that will be in common use by police forces in the years to come. Metts notes that, "In the past, a policeman was given a badge and a gun and told to hit the streets. But tomorrow's super cops will have an array of sophisticated devices with which to do their job."

Among the futuristic police devices—many are already in use—are the laser gun, a weapon that stuns a victim with electrical shock without causing permanent injury or leaving external signs of body damage, light guns, and electronic restraints. Robots are also being put to use. Novel devices include the "space bucket" and "jet pack" which will allow a police officer to soar above and around congestion and hover only a few feet above the ground. "Computer networks," says Metts, "will provide birth-to-death dossiers, giving officers immediate field information."

BRAIN MACHINES

Although the futuristic police equipment described above is being developed for worthwhile purposes, its abuse by a government less democratic than that of today's democracies could bring terror to a beleaguered populace. However, there are other devices now being studied that hold the potential for such monumental abuse that it is reasonable to ask if experimentation should be allowed to continue. I refer to "brain machines"—proposed devices that can be hooked up to or coupled with a person's brain to alter that person's thinking processes.

Dr. Jose Delgado, a Spanish neuroscientist and researcher, is experimenting with brain machines. In one experiment, he implanted electrodes in the brain of a one-thousand-pound bull. As the huge beast lunged at Delgado, the scientist used a radio signal to activate the electrodes in the animal's brain, whereupon the bull came to a sudden halt.

Delgado and other researchers have discovered that electromagnetic fields can seriously disrupt and otherwise affect brain activity and the body's nervous system. Under the influence of varying electromagnetic fields, some monkeys have been successfully commanded to fall asleep while others were made to become hyperactive and restless.

The Soviet Union is hard at work to harness the power of microwaves and other electromagnetic fields to influence the behavior of human beings. Soviet scientists have even constructed a machine that bombards a person's brain from long distance with radio waves, producing tranquilized or trancelike states. Such machines are also being tested currently at a United States Veterans Administration hospital.

In their book *The Mind Race,* scientists Russell Targ and Keith Harary outlined some of the research under way in the Soviet Union—research actually described to the authors by the Soviet scientists themselves. In one experiment, the Soviets induced heart attacks in rats with electromagnetic generators; in another, a device put an entire hall full of people to sleep in fifteen minutes. Even more ominous was the use of an electronic oscillator. When brought near human patients' heads by the researchers, the instrument apparently caused the patients to have "mystical or religious types of experiences."[2]

In the United States and elsewhere, it has been demonstrated that electrical impulses fed into specific regions of the brain's cerebral cortex can radically alter personality. In experiments, a cat became terrified at the mere sight of a mouse and an unfriendly, vicious monkey became friendly and gentle.

"Dream machines" once were a popular topic of science fiction writers, but today such machines— attached to the human brain with electrodes or possibly implanted on a microchip—are on the threshold of becoming reality. In *What Sort of People Should There Be?* British scientist Jonathan Glover discusses the frightening implications of such machines. He remarks that a dream machine could be developed that will stimulate the brain so that a person has a sequence of enjoyable experiences. These pleasurable images would seem so real they would be indistinguishable from the equivalent real-life experiences. (A machine that could generate such sensations was the subject of the film *Brainstorm*.)

Glover suggests that for some people, the dream machine would be an opiate, providing experiences so pleasurable that individuals would actually prefer remaining hooked to the machine to experiencing real life with all its tragedies and disappointments. The very thought of this revolts most of us, but Glover also describes the ultimate horror: the compulsory plugging of a person's brain into a "nightmare" machine:

> Consider a machine . . . called the Horror Machine. It starts by banging your head against a wall, so that you have an intense desire for this to stop. . . . Next, it plunges you under water, giving you an intense desire to surface before you drown. . . .[3]

The thought of being threatened with a lifetime on such a machine would induce sheer terror in a person's mind. Never in human history have tyrants and madmen had such tools—tools which they can use to terrorize an individual or an entire population.

Future technological advances will surely provide such mind control tools. G. Harry Stine, in *Silicon Gods*, predicts that, very soon, intelligence amplifiers—tiny microchip devices either implanted in humans or capable of being temporarily connected to the human brain and sensory channels—will actually allow others to "get inside a person's head." With such devices, we will possess the astonishing ability to hear the thoughts of others.[4]

Researchers are making rapid progress to bring this to reality. A recent article in *Science News* reported that "new electronic techniques are being developed to eavesdrop on the brain." The techniques, under study at the University of Michigan at Ann Arbor, in AT & T labs, and elsewhere, may allow outsiders to direct a person's brain cell conversations and talk directly to the individual's brain neurons. Current research centers on the eventual employment of integrated circuit chips that can be either implanted in the brain or overlaid with brain cells.[5]

One shudders to think of the power this capability might give corrupt leaders or thugs bent on controlling the mind-thoughts of individuals. Stine, an optimist who believes that man will not allow the abuse of these capabilities, nevertheless warns:

> It also contains the seeds of unimaginable evil: the actual control of human minds by other hu-

mans. Not brain-washing. Not propaganda. Not any of the ancient and well-proven means of mentally or physically imposing one person's will by police action or torture. But the actual control of the human mind.[6]

TOMORROW'S GESTAPO

Parade magazine, in its February 23, 1986, issue, profiled Elie Wiesel, the courageous survivor of Nazi concentration camps. Wiesel, who won the Nobel Peace Prize in 1986, was a boy of only thirteen when he and his entire family became victims of the Gestapo. His parents perished. At a public school, young American students asked Wiesel about his dreadful experiences. "Can you describe the look in people's eyes when they did what they did to you?" asked one intense young man.

Wiesel answered sadly, "No, they behaved, they acted as gods. We victims could not look into the faces of gods, the faces of the killers. I only remember the eyes of the victims."

Elie Wiesel pleaded with the students to remember the Nazi holocaust so that it could never be repeated. But, in examining the newest tech tools that could be available to the future successors of yesterday's Nazi "gods," we must understand that the seeds of a technological nightmare have already been planted. These seeds could well bear cruel fruit in the dark days of the Antichrist. One shudders to think what tomorrow might bring as scientists in the employ of what might be the most cruel and energetic secret police in history crank out a succession of terrifying instruments.

Many people discount the possibility of future abuse of these tech tools. They depict an alternative future in which the human potential for good will be realized. Given a choice, they say, man will do good. To think otherwise, they contend, is negative thought.

But listen to the troubled words of Elie Wiesel, a sober man who knows much more than most of us about the evil that dwells beneath the surface in so many people. When asked by a young questioner if, perhaps, the Germans who committed atrocities in the concentration camps had no choice but to carry out the orders of superiors, Wiesel calmly responded:

> The killer has a choice. Every human being has the same choice. Some of the Nazis were highly educated persons. Some of them went home at night and read poetry. Yes, a killer chooses to be a killer.

Wiesel understands, as Christians do, that man is a creature responsible for his moral choices. Men consciously choose to abuse technology and to kill other human beings. As we will scc in Part III, the choice to kill—or to prepare to kill—is a choice being made by more and more government leaders. In spite of Wiesel's sobering words, it appears that man at the end of the twentieth century is determined to outdo the Nazi holocaust, both in the number of persons killed and in the technical expertise of killing.

PART TWO

And Hell Followed With Him

SIX
THE WEAPONS AND
WARRIORS
OF ARMAGEDDON

Shortly after observing the carnage and misery of
World War I, inventor Thomas Alva Edison made a
prediction:

> There will one day spring from the brain of sci-
> ence a machine or force so fearful in its potenti-
> alities, so absolutely terrifying that even man the
> fighter, who will dare torture and death in order
> to inflict torture and death, will be appalled. . . .

On August 6, 1945, the prediction of Edison was
borne out, for on that day the fruits of man's advances
in war power came into clear focus. Early that morning
a B-29 bomber nicknamed *Enola Gay* dropped a nine-
thousand-pound bomb dubbed "Little Boy" on the unsuspecting city of Hiroshima. The awesome explosion
which followed leveled nearly every structure in the
Japanese city, melted cobblestones, and killed or

wounded almost eighty thousand people. The world had entered the nuclear age.

The specter of World War III has haunted mankind ever since that horrible day in 1945 when the first atomic bomb caused such overwhelming destruction. General Douglas MacArthur aptly described this sentiment when he stated, "Modern war is ugly . . . a creation of Satan."

The twentieth century has seen astonishing advances in military weaponry. Only eighty-two years ago—about one human life span—Orville and Wilbur Wright brought to reality a primitive flying machine. The battle tank found its first real use in World War I, while nuclear bombs, strategic bombers, and aircraft carriers came into their own some forty-five years ago during World War II. Since 1945, further advances have been made. These include the development of intercontinental ballistic missiles tipped with multiple warheads and the introduction of "smart" bombs and tactical missiles during the Vietnam and Middle East conflicts.

However, as remarkable as all these advances in weaponry have been, the next generation of military weapons—now in production or on the drawing boards—will eclipse anything we have today. By the early dawn of the twenty-first century, a quantum leap in technological sophistication and lethality will have been achieved as a vast array of mind-boggling tools of war are added to military arsenals.

THE NEW HIGH-TECH ARSENAL

The newest tools of armed conflict are frighteningly reminiscent of those seen in *Star Wars* and *Buck Rog-*

ers movies. If this sounds like an overstatement, take a look at some of man's new life-destroying military weapons. Each of these is either available now or will be in a few years.

- "Smart" bombs—called precision guided munitions—that *take themselves* directly to a minute, well-hidden target.
- "Stealth" aircraft, armed with nuclear bombs, that are invisible to radar.
- Laser beams that cut holes in airplanes and can even cause supersonic aircraft and speeding missiles to disintegrate or vaporize in flight.
- Computerized robots dexterous and rugged enough to help or replace soldiers in combat.
- Charged energy weapons, operated from space platforms, that can project a deadly ray to earth to irradiate hundreds of miles of territory.
- Neutron bombs that can kill men and women with poisonous radiation, yet leave buildings, vehicles, and other property intact.
- Biological toxins, delivered by aircraft and missiles, that can blanket an entire nation with odious epidemics of cholera, yellow fever, and a score of other infectious diseases.
- Chemical weapons which induce terror or hallucinations in an enemy's armies and population.
- Drugs that cause soldiers to believe they are invincible "super-warriors." Also, drugs that

diminish or eliminate guilt feelings of soldiers ordered to commit atrocities.

These are only a few of the destructive weapons we know either exist at present or which will be added to existing arsenals. They sound like science fiction toys created to excite the imaginations of young movie-goers or for use in home video games. Instead, they are scientific tools capable of creating a huge swath of destruction and terror.

LIKE MEN IN A DREAM

Commenting on this never-ending growth in the technology of warfare, George Kennan, former ambassador to the Soviet Union and one of the most honored statesmen of our time, stated that "we have gone on piling weapon upon weapon, missile upon missile, new levels of destructiveness upon old ones."

Significantly, Kennan added, "We have done this helplessly, almost involuntarily: like victims of some sort of men in a dream, like lemmings headed for the sea."

Kennan's words are testimony that the hand of Satan is evident in the malignant development of the newer weapons of killing. Without God, man is helpless in stopping the onrushing tide of war. And leaders of nations are being led by the Evil One to marshal all the forces of technology in building terrible weapons of death.

In this chapter and the next, we'll discuss the new armaments. The modern weapons of war and their effects described here were researched from a host of sources: Air Force and Army technical reports and manuals, Department of Defense and Arms Control Agency documents, numerous journal articles, and several excellent books, including *The New High Ground* by Thomas Karas, *The Weapons of World War III* by William J. Koenig, and *How to Make War* by James F. Dunnigan. The knowledge and insight afforded by my own years of experience as a U.S. Air Force officer and professor of defense policy and aerospace studies will also be called upon.

MICROCHIP GENERALS AND STAR WARRIORS: THE NEW MILITARY

As you read of the new instruments of warfare devised by modern science and technology and wonder at their sophistication and lethal powers, keep in mind that these weapons are paralleled by the "new style" flesh-and-blood warriors who wield them. The U.S. military personnel who develop, maintain, and operate today's technological weapons constitute a totally new military force. They represent an amazing transformation that has occurred in our nation's armed forces.

We still have our Marines, our Green Berets, and our paratroopers, and they serve well in times of world tension and regional conflicts. But in an age where the world is but an inch away from nuclear destruction and technological weapons are truly combat marvels, it is the high-tech specialist that is most in demand—and the most valued. Furthermore, in future wars, most killing will be conducted at long range. Missiles, anti-tank rockets, neutron bombs, and other weapons controlled from distances of up to seventy-five miles will be common. The era of hand-to-hand combat and aerial dogfights is ending. Today's major conflicts will be fought without most combatants ever seeing the dead bodies of their victims.

The high-tech revolution in our armed forces is dramatically changing leadership patterns. Present-day generals and admirals do not at all resemble those of the precomputer age. All have college degrees, most at the graduate level, and increasingly in a technical discipline. Promising officers with doctorates in scientific curricula are now being assigned to significant positions of responsibility in charge of high-tech military projects.

A first example of this new high-tech warrior leader was Gen. Lew Allen, appointed U.S. Air Force Chief of Staff in 1978. Holder of a Ph.D. in physics, Allen, whose previous job was commander of Systems Command—the Air Force's top research organization— promptly reoriented the service's recruiting and promotion policies to favor science and engineering personnel and boosted scientific research activities. Although he has since retired, Allen's successors have continued his policies.

Today, with multibillion dollar research budgets and an army of scientists and engineers, the armed forces are at the vanguard of the high-tech revolution. Military research is being conducted in virtually every area of high technology, from bioengineering to robotics.

For example, take the role of the Pentagon's DARPA in the development of huge, number-crunching supercomputers. DARPA (Defense Advanced Research Proj-

ects Agency) has been called by *Newsweek* magazine
the premier world computer research organization. According to *Newsweek:*

> More than any other single agency in the world,
> [DARPA] is responsible for the shape of ad-
> vanced computer science today—and for many
> technologies now in widespread commercial use.

The first supercomputer built (1964) was a DARPA
achievement, and computer graphics is a DARPA-
sponsored creation. DARPA is now directing an advanced artificial intelligence project and building an incredible supercomputer system to process information
at blistering speeds.

The Soviet Union also has its technological warriors.
The military gets the lion's share of economic resources from the Kremlin and has built up a technological combat force superior to that of the United
States in a number of significant areas. Like U.S. military personnel, the new-style Soviet general, admiral,
lower echelon officer, or soldier is a product of the
technological era.

Indications are that the people element will continue
to evolve as newer technologies are adopted by the Soviet and U.S. armed forces. Military training budgets
are increasing rapidly, and biological scientists are even
now working to prepare the human species for the next
world war. In *U.S. News & World Report* (May 9,
1983), it was stated that "as warfare becomes more lethal, combatants will be forced to change." According
to the magazine, soldiers will probably be immunized

against stress and will be able to fight for weeks without sleep.

In other sources, new drugs under development are detailed, drugs which could be used to inoculate soldiers against fear and which reduce or eliminate guilt feelings resulting from killing other human beings. Credible news reports claim that Russia has created or is close to creating chemical compounds that induce anger and aggressiveness in humans. Even psychic methods of warfare, including mind control, are under serious study by military scientists (see chapter 11).

It is frightening to contemplate that in battles to come the horrendous instruments and machines of war may be operated and controlled by American combatants honed as intense fighting machines and by Communist super-warriors who possess little more than a desire to kill, maim, and destroy.

ARE WE APPROACHING A WORLD WAR III ARMAGEDDON?

In his book *Approaching Hoofbeats: The Four Horsemen of the Apocalypse,* Dr. Billy Graham truly demonstrated God-given insight and wisdom when he wrote:

> I hear the hoofbeats of the four horsemen approaching. I hear the thundering approach of false teaching, war, famine and death. I see and hear these signs as a shadow of God's loving hand at work for the world's redemption. God is offering hope for those who heed the warning.[1]

I agree with Dr. Graham. In the succeeding chapters, as we examine many of the incredible new weapons of warfare made possible by scientific progress, prick your own ears forward a bit and listen. Listen to see if you, too, can hear the hoofbeats of the four horsemen of the apocalypse approaching.

SEVEN
THE HORRIBLE PROSPECT: NUCLEAR WAR

Since the atomic bombing of Nagasaki and Hiroshima in 1945, the specter of nuclear war has haunted the earth.* It is difficult not to be alarmed when we examine the grim statistics of nuclear armament. Twenty-five years ago, the United States had about 250 nuclear missiles, the USSR less than 50. Today, each nation has more than 2,000 nuclear missiles, including those on land (ICBMs) and in submarines (SLBMs). And that's not all! Many of these missiles can accommodate several nuclear warheads—the Soviet's largest missile carries up to ten—giving modern missilery an unmatched capacity for destruction.

But of course, this is only the missiles. Nuclear weapons also are launched from strategic bombers and

---

*In 1961, the Soviet Union exploded a monstrous fifty-megaton nuclear weapon. This weapon had four thousand times the destructive power of the bomb dropped on Hiroshima!

tactical aircraft. Pentagon figures show that together the two superpowers—the U.S. and the USSR—possess in their combined arsenals a frightening total of nearly fifty thousand nuclear arms. And the total is growing.

NUCLEAR WEAPONS PROLIFERATE

In his 1982 report on military posture, the chairman of the Joint Chiefs of Staff, Gen. David Jones, USAF, called the 1980s "the dangerous decade ahead." Blaming the spread of nuclear arms, the report stated that "the nuclear umbrella is darker and more extensive than ever before."

In the previous ten years, cited the report:

- The warhead count had gone up 200 percent,
- Explosive power had grown some 30 percent, and
- Hard target kill potential had increased 200 percent.

Today, it is known that eight countries—the U.S., the Soviet Union, Britain, France, China, Israel, South Africa, and India—possess nuclear weapons. However, in 1982, a Defense Department intelligence survey found that thirty-one countries, many engaged in longstanding regional disputes, will be able to produce nuclear weapons by the year 2000.

Take Pakistan, for example. An impoverished nation with starving masses that can ill afford the expense, Pakistan is now on the verge of developing a nuclear bomb. Why? After Pakistan's hated neighbor, India, exploded its own atomic bomb in the 1970s, the Pakistani leader, Ali Bhutto, stated belligerently that "we will starve, we will eat grass if we have to, but we will develop our own atomic bombs." If the Hindus of India have this monstrous weapon, reasoned Bhutto, then the Muslims of Pakistan shall as well.

THE EFFECTS OF NUCLEAR WEAPONS

What damage to property and loss of life would result if the world's fifty thousand nuclear weapons were exploded? It's too horrible to even measure. In his book *Weapons of World War III,*[1] defense analyst William J. Koenig says that if *only five hundred* nuclear weapons were detonated—a mere 1 percent of those stockpiled—the following results would occur:

- 50 million people would die instantly. Many more—as much as the entire population of Europe and half of that of the U.S. and the Soviet Union—would die later from radiation sickness and epidemics of cholera, typhus, cancer, and other diseases spawned in the aftermath of the explosion.
- Changes in climate would result, with many people suffering fatal sunburn and skin diseases caused by the destruction of much of the earth's ozone layer and the subsequent exposure to the sun's deadly ultraviolet rays.

Imagine the devastation to cities and industry if, as Dr. Koenig speculates, only 1 percent of the available nuclear warheads were unleashed. Surely this would be an apocalyptic event which modern man can't even begin to contemplate. But then, consider the toll that would result from an *all-out nuclear war*. In 1983, a World Health Organization report by a committee of ten scientists calculated that such a war would leave in its aftermath 2 billion victims—that's nearly half the world's population of 4.5 billion. The survivors could not expect medical attention, and millions would starve. Perhaps, as Premier Nikita Khruschev of the Soviet Union once said, "The survivors of nuclear war will envy the dead."

The primary effects of nuclear weaponry are as follows: savage winds, mushroom cloud, a raging fire that enfolds and billows its fireball, and a blinding flash. After the initial blast, the specter of radiation awaits survivors.

Fire and Heat. One of the most damaging aspects of nuclear weapons is the fierce heat generated upon detonation. An ultrahot, rapidly expanding fireball consumes virtually everything in its path. This blast of heat is no respecter of property or persons: homes, buildings, people, animals—all would be incinerated as the fire, heat, and flash move across the land. A small (one-megaton) explosion would cause severe third-degree burns up to five miles away.

Blast. Casualties in a nuclear war obviously mount from the effects of the blast. The energy released, first heard as a loud, highly charged noise, can best be conceived of as a shock wave, a wave of magnified, compressed air. This air has the destructive force of a deadly hurricane as it sweeps along at supersonic speed, destroying practically everything it encounters. A small nuclear weapon can generate winds of 250 miles per hour, about as much as a tornado, while a larger weapon can send forth winds at an awesome velocity of over 700 miles per hour.

According to Koenig, such dynamic pressure "makes twigs, pebbles, broken glass and other small objects as deadly as shrapnel and can also hurl people against hard surfaces with lethal effects." However, most of the casualties would result from collapsing structures.

In 1979, the Office of Technology Assessment of the U.S. Congress conducted a study that showed blast effects of a single, one-megaton bomb on a city. If Detroit was the target, said the study, the blast would dig a crater in downtown Detroit 200 feet deep and 1,000 feet across. Nearly all structures in a 5.4 mile radius would be destroyed; 220,000 people would die and the total casualties would be over one million—all this from one bomb. Yet experts say that in a major war, targeted cities could expect over a dozen such warheads!

A Shaking of the Earth. Another characteristic effect of a nuclear explosion is that observers experience it as earthshaking. Witnesses to nuclear tests have stated how, miles distant from ground zero, they felt the earth move with tremors. Said one man, over fifty miles away from a blast, "I thought it was an earthquake; the earth appeared to shift. It truly frightened me." Experts also say that, following a nuclear explosion, there is a danger of secondary quakes as the earth and its numerous earthquake fault lines react to the violence of the blast.

In Isaiah 14:16-17, the prophet speaks of an evil figure who "made the earth to tremble, that did shake kingdoms; that made the world as a wilderness, and destroyed the cities thereof." Likewise, in 24:18 Isaiah envisions that the "foundations of the earth do shake" and in the same chapter, verse 20, he gives us an image of the predicament that will result when thousands of thermonuclear weapons are exploded in the fury of world war: "The earth shall reel to and fro like a drunkard, and shall be removed like a cottage."

These words of Isaiah appear to warn mankind of another danger involved in nuclear war that is even more scary than quakes and tremors, as damaging as they may be. Some scientists contend that an all-out exchange of nuclear weapons will cause a shifting of the poles of the earth. Geological evidence indicates that during prehistoric times, there were many reversals of geographical poles. Such shifting caused cataclysmic upheavals—seas flooding entire continents, plains thrust into mountains, civilizations razed to rubble, and towering forests made into scattered debris.

It seems likely, then, that massive blasts of spasmodic nuclear attacks could result in earthquakes, volcanoes, enormous shifting of mountains and hills, and gigantic tidal waves. Entire continents could disappear beneath the sea. Multiple nuclear blasts could break dams, change the course of rivers, and topple great cities.

In a foreword to the book *The Path of the Pole* (by Charles Hapgood), Albert Einstein affirmed the possibility of a shifting of the earth's geographical poles. Furthermore Einstein, whose work laid the foundation for development of the atomic bomb, stated that it would not take much of an impact for such a dreadful event to occur. "Such displacements," said Einstein, "may take place as the consequence of comparatively slight forces exerted on the crust, derived from the earth's momentum of rotation, which in turn will tend to alter the axis of rotation of the earth's crust."[2]

Blackout. Another effect of nuclear explosion is the phenomenon known as electromagnetic pulse (EMP). EMP waves are much like radio waves but many thousands of times stronger—so strong that they disrupt and severely damage communications and electric power systems. This, in turn, produces a blackout in the affected area: the elimination of radio, television, electric lights, utilities, and perhaps even telephone lines. Everything powered by electricity will grind to a halt. Darkness will envelop the land. Authorities say that a single atomic bomb, detonated high in the atmosphere, could knock out electricity over the entire United States.

Dust. As if the effects of EMP would not be enough, nuclear scientists believe that the blasts of scores of nuclear explosions would throw huge amounts of dust into the upper atmosphere. This would fulfill the Bible's prophecy that, in the time of tribulation, the sun will be darkened and the earth plunged into blackness:

> And it shall come to pass in that day, saith the Lord God, that I will cause the sun to go down at noon, and I will darken the earth in the clear day. (Amos 8:9)

Imagine the fear and trepidation that would grip humanity as electrical power fails. Minor blackouts in the 1960s in New York City and on the East Coast caused panic and pandemonium. Soon, just a few years from now, the entire United States—probably the whole world—could experience an eerie *total* blackout as thousands of tons of dust obscure the sun and usher in a period of darkness. First would come the initial flash of the fireball, melting the very eyeballs of those who observe it close-up; then electromagnetic radiation and dust will extinguish the light.

Radiation. One of the deadly effects of nuclear weapons is the harmful radiation that results. This radiation travels rapidly through the air. If a bomb is exploded near clouds or over a body of water, poisonous rain showers may fall on people, property, and land. Radiation can kill immediately, or within days, weeks, or months, depending on the dose.

The most terrifying aspect of radiation is the *manner* in which it kills. Often the process is slow and painful, and the victim of radiation sickness suffers greatly. Agonizing deaths can result from delayed poisoning or from the outright battering the blood, lungs, and brain suffer from ingestion of excess radiation. Exposed victims who live for longer periods may be stricken with cancer of all kinds and with leukemia—harrowing effects, points out William Koenig, that leave people "tainted with deformity and death."

According to Koenig, the radiation fallout area following the detonation of a single nuclear device may be up to two hundred miles long and twenty-five miles wide. Fishermen eighty miles away from a test blast over Bikini Atoll in 1954 in the Pacific came down with serious illnesses from radiation poisoning, and one died.

Not only does a nuclear explosion cover a wide area with radiation poison, but the body-destroying effect of this ghastly chemical lingers for a long, long time, perhaps exerting its abhorrent effects months and even years after the blast. Small traces of radiation fallout from above-ground nuclear tests in 1963 still are being detected over twenty years later!

THE REAL NUCLEAR THREAT

Examining these facts leads us to wonder if all-out nuclear war could really happen. Is humanity doomed to extinction? The man often called the "Father of the atomic bomb," Albert Einstein, once pondered such questions. The great scientist finally came to the conclusion that it is not the bomb we must fear, but human beings with empty souls who hold the power to unleash nuclear terror. Einstein asked: "What is it that we really fear? Is it the power of the atom bomb or is it the force of evil within the heart of man?"

EIGHT
TERROR FROM THE HEAVENS: SPACE AND AIR WARFARE

The development by the superpowers of massive air and space combat forces has long been a top priority. Each nation's military force now includes a wide range of systems, from supersonic jet fighter aircraft packed with electronic gadgetry to nuclear-bomb-carrying intercontinental ballistic missiles (ICBMs). In recent years, space systems have been emphasized, and billions of dollars are now being spent on lasers, particle beam weapons, and other ultrasophisticated arms designed to attack targets *in* space and targets on earth *from* space.

SPACE WAR

In 1962, newspaper columnist Stewart Alsop wrote that "man will use the fourth dimension of space as he has used the earth, the sea, and the air—to assert his power, to make his will prevail, perhaps to make war on other men." More recently, in 1982, Undersecretary of the Air Force Edward C. Aldridge asserted that "our use of space in support of our military forces is inevitable—the advantages are clear."

In the early 1960s, President John F. Kennedy encouraged the peaceful use of space and even negotiated a treaty with Moscow to ban weapons in space. But since the days of Hitler's V-2 rockets, Russia's Sputnik satellite, and the U.S. moon shot, many other military and political leaders have held the same view as Alsop and Aldridge: the militarization of space is inevitable.

The huge expenditures over the past decade by the Soviet Union on space weapons far exceeds the amounts spent by the United States. In its FY 85 report to the Congress, the U.S. Air Force noted that "the Soviets are busy exploiting space for military advantage, including development of an antisatellite weapon." The report also said, "Since Sputnik in 1957, the Soviets have launched twice as many spacecraft as the United States, and 85 percent of their space activities are related to military efforts."[1] Because of the advantage sought by the USSR, there is little chance, if any, of stemming the tide of weaponry being produced to patrol the heavens.

Among the space systems now in use or proposed for use are the following:

- A comprehensive system of weather and communications satellites.
- Spy and surveillance satellites that gather intelligence and also detect hostile intercontinental ballistic missiles shortly after launch.
- America's NAVSTAR Global Positioning Satellite System, with precise atomic clocks designed to improve accuracy of sea-based

nuclear-tipped missiles and to enhance military operations by providing minute and accurate position information.

● Project High Frontier, a proposal of Lt. Gen. Daniel O. Graham (Ret.) and others to build a defensive system of 432 satellites in space. This system would detect Soviet missiles and fire charges to destroy them in flight.

● The continued use by the superpowers of space shots for military missions, including testing and eventual development of lasers, particle beams, and other weapons on space stations and other space platforms.

● America's initial antisatellite (ASAT) force, scheduled to be in place by 1987, consisting of twenty-eight modified F-15 aircraft with fifty-six rockets, each designed to intercept and destroy enemy satellites. The Soviets also are developing an ASAT force and have conducted successful tests.

● Research on a true aerospace plane similar to the space orbiter vehicle that can take off and land on runways instead of launch pads. Called the transatmospheric vehicle (TAV), and capable of speeds of 18,000 miles per hour, this aircraft is being designed by McDonnell-Douglas under a USAF design contract.

● Satellites deployed to detect enemy submarines hidden in the ocean depths, making the Soviet submarine force highly vulnerable to destruction by nuclear depth charges and other new weapons.

- The new, devastatingly powerful electromagnetic railgun, now in prototype stage, which is able to fire projectiles at a quantum velocity and obliterate distant targets in space. Called simply the "electric gun," this weapon can be mounted on unmanned satellites orbiting the earth or on planes and tanks. With machine gun rapidity, it uses huge bursts of electronic energy to fire small projectiles able to destroy much larger space targets, such as missiles, satellites, an opponent's space platform, or ground targets such as trucks or tanks.

Collectively, these systems—known as "Star Wars" in the media—are referred to as Strategic Defense Initiative (SDI) by the U.S. Department of Defense.

DEATH RAYS

In 1976, I was selected by the Air Force to attend a special three-month course at Maxwell Air Force Base, Alabama, designed to train officers for advanced management positions. Special briefing teams were sent from the Pentagon, Headquarters Strategic Air Command, and from the other services to bring the assembled USAF officers up to date on the newest weapon systems in the military arsenals. One of the weapons discussed was the laser.

We were shown a dramatic film of a small drone plane in flight. Suddenly, from the earth, a fixed stream of superheated laser rays struck the plane. For several minutes, as the plane continued to fly on its course, the corrosive and concentrated laser beam focused on the metal of the plane's frame. A hole appeared in the outer metal and soon the plane burst into flames and went crashing to the ground.

All of us in attendance were amazed at the speed of the laser and its ability to actually melt an airplane frame while in flight.

Now, over a decade later, laser ray weapons have been greatly improved. In only a few more years—ten at the most—we undoubtedly will have laser weapons that will beam at the speed of light (186,282 miles per second) toward an incoming enemy missile and obliterate it before it has a chance to begin its downward trajectory.

As Allan Maurer points out in his book *Lasers: The Light Wave of the Future,*[2] since 1960, when a scientist developed the first laser, this technology has been used in a number of wondrous ways. Lasers are now used to drill diamonds, to vaporize cancer, and even to print newspapers. They are also being used to prepare for war.

According to defense consultant William Koenig, the U.S. has already spent over 1.5 billion dollars on development of laser weapons. The Soviet Union has invested three to five times as much.[3] In fact, Maj. Gen. George Keegan, former intelligence chief of the U.S. Air Force, reports that the Soviet Union possesses the world's largest laser weapon and is making a concerted effort to stay ahead of the West. Japan and other nations are also hard at work to develop laser weapon systems.

KILLER BEAMS

Distinguished from the laser beam, the particle beam fires a stream of atomic or subatomic particles, such as electrons, protons, or ions. The particle beam's effect resembles a bolt of lightning.

What kind of destruction can be inflicted with the laser and the particle energy beam? The weapons now envisioned—and under construction—will be able to smash satellites in the sky and bring down enemy missiles and aircraft. On the ground they may turn tanks and armored vehicles into fiery coffins.

Within a decade, powerful energy beams and lasers sitting on space battle stations may be able to direct a heat ray toward an American, British, Middle Eastern, or Soviet city. Such an attack, according to physicists knowledgeable with current research, could incinerate a land area of hundreds of square miles. The first such weapons in space would probably be used defensively to destroy enemy missiles, but their lethality would be so remarkable that their use as offensive weapons would soon take precedence.

Two laser weapon systems already developed and tested are portents of greater and more lethal things to come. The first is a portable system that beams an intense and deadly laser ray back and forth a mile ahead in the path of advancing enemy troops. All who look at the all-encompassing beam would have their optic nerves seared and be permanently blinded. This system, which would be integrated into tanks, helicopters, and small vehicles, is discussed further in chapter 10.

The second laser weapon is a device the U.S. Air Force employs aboard a converted Boeing 747 aircraft called the Airborne Laser Laboratory (ALL). In a 1983 test, the weapon successfully destroyed five air-to-air missiles launched at it. Current research centers on "Coronet Prince," a device affixed to the underside of an aircraft and capable of blinding enemy pilots and damaging the electronic optical systems of enemy aircraft.

ACHIEVING MEGAWAR CAPABILITIES

The United States and the Soviet Union each have the capacity to destroy much—if not all—of modern civilization. Yet, despite the SALT (arms limitation) talks of the 1960s and 1970s and the talks at Geneva, both superpowers continue to add to their arsenals of nuclear weapons and delivery systems. Megawar weapons possessed by the two superpowers include strategic bomber aircraft, submarine-launched ballistic missiles, land-based ICBMs, and cruise missiles.

During the 1970s, the Soviet Union embarked on a major campaign to build and deploy new strategic weapons while the United States strategic forces improved only marginally. As a result, the Soviets now appear to have a definite advantage over the United States and are alarmingly close to a first strike destruction capability. The Soviet Union developed three new types of ICBMs, two new sea-launched ballistic missile systems, a new long-range bomber, and three new classes of nuclear-equipped submarines. In contrast, during this same period the U.S. did not develop any new ICBM systems and deployed only one new type of sea-launched cruise missile and one submarine. Currently, the Soviet Union has more strategic systems under development.

Department of Defense figures reveal that as of 1985, the Soviet ICBM force was comprised of 1,398 launchers carrying almost 6,000 warheads with a tonnage (throw weight) four times the U.S. ICBM force.

In its FY 85 Report to Congress, the U.S. Air Force ominously concluded: "Using only a small portion of their ICBM force, the Soviets could destroy most of our current ICBMs in a first strike. Second, the Soviets have hardened their ICBM silos, command posts, and other significant military leadership facilities to the point that our current missiles have only limited capability against them."[4]

Nuclear-tipped cruise missiles now being deployed are equipped with electronic cameras—eyes—programmed to view the terrain and the target ahead. These eyes lock in and guide the missile to the intended target.

The accuracy of ICBM nuclear missiles is such that the newer missiles can be launched from Montana (or from Byelorussia in the Soviet Union) and travel thousands of miles around the world to strike a target the size of a football field. They can also be launched from submarines stealthily waiting in the oceans.

COMMAND OF THE SKIES

The armed services of the superpowers have big plans for future aircraft. These plans are intended to gain superiority in air combat and insure command of the skies. Each nation has under development new super fighters and improved transport aircraft. They are also infusing existing and future aircraft with robotic controls and sophisticated computer and electronic technologies. Also under way are research and production programs for more accurate air-to-air and air-to-ground tactical missiles equipped with laser and infrared sensors that lock onto and go after moving targets. New war helicopters are also under development—swift ve-

hicles that launch rockets and armor-piercing shells
that can easily destroy tanks and buildings.

Today's sleek jet aircraft, such as the United States's
F-15 and F-16, employ deadly accurate air-to-ground
missiles that scream ahead at supersonic speeds toward
a building many miles distant. These missiles can enter
a specific *window* of the building selected. The pilot of
the attacking aircraft makes his selection with the aid of
a video screen, which receives its picture from the
camera located on the nose of the missile.

Doubters should consider the phenomenal success of
the radar-guided Exocet missile during the Falklands
crisis. An Exocet was fired by an Argentine pilot at the
British destroyer *Sheffield*. Launched miles away, before the ultramodern ship was even in sight of the Argentine plane, the Exocet missile sank the *Sheffield* to
the bottom of the sea. And newer missiles are more accurate—and more lethal—than the Exocet.

At the conclusion of the last chapter we quoted Albert
Einstein, who remarked that the real danger of atomic
weaponry was not that the bomb itself is inherently
evil, but that man has so much evil in his heart. Likewise, the technology that helps us create lasers, particle
beams, and high-speed aircraft is not evil—but human
beings without God are, and so we face the prospect of
global war that not only features nuclear weapons but
also weapons that were, not so long ago, the stuff of
comic book writers. Comic books amuse, but the prospect of soldiers—or worse, civilians—being blinded
by a sweeping laser beam is not amusing. Knowing
that such weapons exist is a grim reminder of human
sin. In spite of what the so-called progressives may

say, human morals have not advanced much, though technology has. In fact, it appears that with the passing of centuries we have only learned new ways to be brutal.

It should be mentioned here that this brutality is not something that awaits the ultimate showdown between the USSR and the United States. War goes on constantly around the globe and, regrettably, it seems to affect the poor Third World countries worse than the (supposedly) more advanced nations of Europe and America. As we will see in the beginning of the next chapter, hellish methods of war are already in wide use, often against the least technologically developed people. This should not surprise us, for human sin is certainly not going to wait until the battle of Armageddon to be unleashed.

NINE
INVISIBLE AGENTS OF DEATH: CHEMICAL AND BIOLOGICAL WARFARE

The H'mong hill people of the tiny village in Laos did not know at first what the airplane had dropped out of the sky. Whatever it was began to spray out pale yellow smoke, which sifted slowly throughout the village. A young girl sitting in a thatched hut told her mother that she could not see well—her vision was blurred. Then her nose began to bleed profusely, and she was overcome with a wave of nausea. She cried out to her mother for help, but by that time her mother had begun to feel the same symptoms. From outside and from the other primitive dwellings was heard the sound of people wailing and screaming in panic.

This particular chemical attack left its victims with severe respiratory problems, diarrhea, bloody stool, and cramping. Many lost consciousness and some died. After death, their bodies turned blue-black and rapidly decomposed. U.S. scientists couldn't find a clue as to what chemical caused such symptoms. The date: August 7, 1975.

According to Dr. Gideon Regalado, head of the Ban Vinai refugee camp in Thailand, the appalling attack on the H'mong people was not unusual. Dr. Regalado, as of 1981, had examined thousands of Laotian refugees who had fled to neighboring Thailand. As reported later in the *Wall Street Journal* of October 15, 1982, Dr. Regalado reported to the United Nations his belief that "lethal chemical weapons have been used regularly on the H'mong communities in Laos."

Who was the perpetrator of this atrocity? According to the U.S. State Department and a host of other authorities, it was the Soviet Union. In his book *Yellow Rain: A Journey Through the Terror of Chemical Warfare,* Sterling Seagrave, a longtime foreign news correspondent, provides convincing evidence that the Soviet Union furnished the Communist government of Laos with the necessary chemical materials to carry out their pernicious assault on the H'mong, a people who opposed the Communist regime.[1]

In December 1980, an ABC news documentary also produced evidence of poisonous gas use in Laos. ABC had an independent laboratory analyze a sample of a yellowish powder dropped from an airplane by the Communists. The lab reported that the sample contained four highly poisonous mycotoxins.

This death from above—Russian style—was also used on the courageous rebels in Afghanistan who opposed the Soviet assault on that nation, which borders the vital Middle East oil belt. The rebel bands and their families in countless villages were regularly the victims of Soviet air chemical barrages that left people vomiting blood, their skin burning. The U.S. State Department has repeatedly protested the USSR's deadly use of chemicals as a violation of international law and agreements. Still, the carnage continues.

In a news conference February 19, 1985, at Washington, D.C.'s Hilton Hotel hosted by the Committee for a Free Afghanistan, Brigadier Rahmatullah Safi, an Afghan freedom fighter, described the carnage inflicted on Afghanistan's people by Soviet chemical and biological warfare. He told of mycotoxins and "yellow rain" attacks, of the explosion of chemical incendiary bombs, and of the release into the air of poisonous spider venom weapons. The latter weapons were said to be hideous in their effects because a person's flesh actually began to rot away after contact. Safi's allegations have been verified by investigations of the U.S. State and Defense Departments as well as independent news sources.

HOW MUCH A THREAT?

Chemical and biological warfare looms ominously in humankind's future. How widespread would such a conflict be? Would the superpowers hesitate to use lethal chemicals in war? Dixy Lee Ray, former head of the Nuclear Regulatory Commission, stated on CNN's "Crossfire" (September 16, 1984), "Everyone is frightened of nuclear weapons, but the danger of chemical and biological weapons is infinitely worse . . . and few people know about it."

The tragedy at Bhopal, India, in 1984 when a cloud of poisonous gas was released after an accident at a chemical factory is evidence of what might happen in a future war. In a nightmare come true, over two thousand persons were left dead and one hundred thousand injured. Streets were strewn with human bodies and animal carcasses, and blinded persons roamed the alleys begging for medical attention. Yet the poisons released in Bhopal that horrible day would amount to only a tiny, almost insignificant amount when compared to the thousands of tons of chemical weapons now stored by military powers and awaiting use.

In the following pages, we'll examine a few of the dangerous chemical and biological weapons that have been developed and are now ready for use in armed conflict. But keep in mind that little I say can truly describe the magnitude of the horror that would result from a general war in which the adversaries go all-out to destroy their opponents with the use of such weapons. And as each day passes, more lethal and more revolting substances are invented.

THE DEVELOPMENT OF CHEMICAL-BIOLOGICAL WEAPONS

Chemical weapons were first used in World War I with incredibly successful results. Opposing forces on the western front employed chemical weapons, and the death toll and human casualties swiftly mounted. The ugly scars and hideous effects of these weapons were held to be so terrible that Hitler, during World War II, refused to employ chemical gases against advancing Allied troops because he feared retaliation in kind.

Chemical weapons should be distinguished from their biological counterparts. Chemical weapons include nerve gases, mustard gases, and other toxic substances. They are chemicals—similar to drugs—that perform the vile task of killing people. Often they attack human bodies the same way insecticides invade and destroy the bodies of flies and mosquitoes. A tiny drop of some nerve gases is sufficient to cause death. The affected person's muscle system goes into a series of violent, involuntary contractions, and the respiratory system fails. The victim is thus asphyxiated to death as his body twitches and shakes—a very unpleasant and unsightly death.

Biological agents, on the other hand, are even more insidious and terrifying. Here we include virulent bacteria and germs. These destructive microbes attack man by spreading infection and disease. Assault with such weapons is more commonly called *germ warfare.*

INVISIBLE KILLERS

Biological warfare agents can spread a vast array of debilitating sickness and disease. On the list are such diseases as anthrax, botulism, cholera, dengue fever, encephalitis, dysentery, bubonic plague, Q fever, Rocky Mountain spotted fever, influenza, smallpox, typhoid, typhus, and yellow fever—quite a rogue's gallery.

Both chemical and biological weapons can be delivered on an unsuspecting populace by canisters mounted on missiles, dropped from airplanes, or fired from long-range artillery. They can also be detonated by saboteurs or terrorist squads. The substances released are often odorless, colorless, and nondetectable. They can be ingested into the lungs or through the skin or eyes. Once contracted, there are few effective antidotes for many of these agents, and in any event, a severe incapacitating illness is virtually assured.

Even if effective medical treatment and antidotes were available, if a massive attack occurred involving the entire United States landmass, available supplies of treatment drugs and antidotes would be quickly exhausted. And it may also be noted that both the U.S. and the USSR are reputed to have developed new strains of bacteria, resistant to any antidote or treatment known to exist.

Could a nation such as the U.S. be overcome by chemical-biological onslaught? Yes, answers Maj. Gen. Marshall Stubbs, a former U.S. Army Chief Chemical Officer. According to Stubbs, biological agents can be disseminated in such a way as to totally blanket a large country or even a whole continent.

A recent book by Jeremy Paxman and Robert Harris, *A Higher Form of Killing: The Secret Story of Gas and Germ Warfare,* also affirms the massive kill potential of these weapons, offering many poignant examples and facts.[2]

Furthermore, in February 1984, the National Security Council delivered a report to President Ronald Reagan warning of dramatic Russian breakthroughs in biological warfare. Based on classified CIA reports, the report flatly stated that the Soviets had the capability to incapacitate or destroy entire populations. The National Security Council warned that the Soviets "have developed gene-splicing techniques as ominous as the atom-splitting discoveries that led to the nuclear bomb." The frightening Soviet achievement results from their work with genetic engineering techniques. One new biotech gas developed by Russia, a supervirus, can actually attack and destroy the human brain.

At this moment, in laboratories in the Soviet Union and other major world powers, biotechnologists, chemists, and other scientists are studying new substances as potential weaponry for chemical and biological warfare. Many new agents have been discovered as by-products of otherwise harmless research by drug manufacturers and university research centers. For example, the Johns Hopkins School of Medicine in Baltimore, Maryland, is currently testing a revolutionary painkiller that, according to reports, may rival aspirin and related compounds and may even be as powerful as morphine.

In working on this painkiller, scientists found that a natural compound called bradykinin is a substance that triggers pain in human nerve cells. Dr. Soloman Snyder, a professor at Johns Hopkins, says that bradykinin "is the most painful substance known to man. If you apply bradykinin you get severe and exquisite pain."[3]

It is reasonable to assume that bradykinin and similar substances may be the focus of research by scientists working for their governments to develop new, more powerful warfare agents.

THINKING THE UNTHINKABLE

No one is safe from this invisible terror from the skies. In the case of biological attack, once the odious organisms are unleashed, common sense tells us that the diseases spawned could rapidly spread throughout the world, killing hundreds of millions of people. One has only to consider the spread of the black death (bubonic plague) in Europe in the fourteenth century, an epidemic that left over 100 million dead—nearly half the population of that day.

The Soviet Union now has a large stockpile of biological weapons, and every year, new and more advanced agents are developed. The Soviets have expended great amounts of money to develop an arsenal of these grotesque tools of war. U.S. laboratories are also working on new biological agents, but under the restriction that their use be only to enable development of antidotes so that U.S. troops will be protected from enemy attack. However, it is only a short step from development to production, and few experts doubt that production will ensue once a war is initiated. U.S. research efforts have increased 54 percent since 1980.

Some 8,500 U.S. armed forces civilian and military personnel work full-time on chemical and biological weapons research, development, production, and deployment. It is estimated that the Soviet Union now employs over 50,000 specialists and technicians in the chemical and biological warfare fields. Both superpowers are providing their military forces increased training in the use of protective gear and clothing, with the expectation that chemical-biological weapons will most certainly be employed in the future.

THE SOVIET ADVANTAGE

James Dunnigan estimates that the U.S. now has forty thousand tons of chemical munitions; the Soviets have even more.[4] Other experts put the U.S. figure at twenty-eight thousand and the Soviet total at a staggering seven hundred thousand tons. China and France also have chemical and biological warfare capabilities. Iraq used chemical weapons against Iranian soldiers several times from 1983 through 1986. It is not known what other nations have these weapons, although the technology for their development is easy to acquire.

As with missiles and nuclear technology, the Soviet Union has forged far ahead of the United States in this arena of war preparedness. Richard L. Wagner, Assistant Secretary to the Secretary of Defense for Atomic Energy, and Theodore S. Gold, the defense department's top official for chemical matters, outlined a few years ago (*Defense* magazine, July 1982) the supremacy of the Soviet armed forces. They revealed that the Soviet army has nineteen chemical training battalions, the U.S. Army only one; the Soviets have stockpiled eleven types of chemical agents, the U.S. just four. Wagner and Gold concluded that "the Soviet Union today possesses a decisive military advantage . . . and thus, there would be an incentive for them to use chemical weapons in future conflicts."

The horrible truth is that in the last days warfare could result in grisly death and suffering for much of mankind. The combined specter of nuclear arms *and* chemical-biological weapons in the hands of evil world leaders is almost too appalling to contemplate.

DAYS OF HUNGER

It is important to keep in mind that these weapons will kill also through indirect means: by depriving populations of food and water. The combined effects of nuclear, chemical, biological, and laser energy warfare would likely leave the earth denuded and the water poisonous and unfit to drink.

Perhaps the most alarming images of world hunger are found in the Book of Revelation. There, in chapter 6, are several frightening references, one of which depicts one of the four horsemen of the apocalypse as the harbinger of death and starvation:

> And I looked, and behold a pale horse: and his name that sat on him was Death, and Hell followed with him. And power was given unto them over the fourth part of the earth, to kill with sword, and with hunger. . . . (Rev. 6:8)

Elsewhere in Revelation, we see that an angel will cast his vial upon the sea, leaving it ruined and extinguishing all sea life (Rev. 16:3).

The net result of the latter-day assaults on the earth's resources is mentioned in Revelation 6:6, where John reports that after the rider of the black horse holds in his hand a pair of balances, a voice is heard saying, "A measure of wheat for a penny, and three measures of barley for a penny." This suggests that the acquisiton of food will become a major preoccupation of man in the days of hunger ushered in by the latter-day weapons of war.

Ezekiel envisioned a day when people will no longer be able to trust in the safety of water and food: "Son of man, eat thy bread with quaking, and drink thy water with trembling and with carefulness" (12:18). City dwellers will especially be plagued; said the prophet: "He that is in the city, famine and pestilence shall devour him" (7:15).

There are two good reasons why Ezekiel's prophetic words may soon be translated into unpleasant reality. First, cities are often prime targets for radioactive nuclear warheads. Second, in the throes of all-out world war, teams of terrorists and saboteurs can be expected to detonate high-level radiation charges and deposit chemical-biological agents in waterways. The result would be dreadful epidemics and sickness as the poisoned water is drunk by people and cattle and used to water agricultural fields.

Ezekiel perhaps expressed this grim, future ruination of water supplies by terrorists when he pointed out that people would "drink their water with astonishment . . . because of the violence of all them that dwell therein" (12:19).

The prophets say that many men will die from hunger, and some will become so desperate that they will mutilate themselves in seeking to satisfy their hunger:

> And he shall snatch on the right hand, and be hungry; and he shall eat on the left hand, and they shall not be satisfied: they shall eat every man the flesh of his own arm. (Isa. 9:20)

Others, driven to murderous acts and sacrilege by lack of food, will turn to the flesh of their fellowmen as the world of the last days devolves into a frantic struggle for survival: "That that dieth, let it die . . . and let the rest eat every one the flesh of another" (Zech. 11:9).

Some Bible scholars believe that these ghastly prophecies warn of symbolic events, or that they are dramatizations. However, when we consider the depraved acts that have historically occurred when men were deprived of food and water, we realize the literal possibilities of these prophecies.

TEN
NO PLACE TO HIDE:
THE WAR BELOW

If the war from above seems ominous, with Star Wars conflict in space and thousands of missiles and aircraft furiously engaged in mortal combat, consider the war below on earth. The technologically advanced nations have developed new tanks, mechanized armor, artillery, and other weapons that will, in the future, greatly magnify the death and destruction experienced in earlier world wars. High-tech electronics have vastly changed the nature of warfare; today, the computer is becoming as essential to victory in battle as the tank and the infantry rifle. New ground weapons employing speed-of-light lasers will greatly increase kill capability, and chemical and biological attacks could decimate entire battalions of troops. Even robots and robotics will play roles in future conflict. Both the superpowers are giving high priority to robot battle machines.

Riding the waves of the seas and concealed deep below the surface in the dark depths of the world's oceans are mighty battle craft equipped with remarkable electronic wizardry and unequalled firepower. As we'll discuss shortly, the U.S. Navy has nuclear-powered, missile-carrying submarines so lethal that the ballistic missiles fired from just one of these submarines could wipe a half dozen of the Soviet Union's largest cities off the map. The Soviet forces also have missile-carrying submarines. Over the past two decades, the Soviet Union has spent billions to equip a huge naval force that now threatens American ships and subs in the Pacific, the Mediterranean, and every major sea-lane on earth.

Traditional weapons such as tanks, helicopters, and aircraft carriers only vaguely resemble their World War II predecessors. Modern tanks—like the West's M-1 Abrams tank—are computerized monsters that shoot armor-piercing shells at targets two-and-a-half miles distant. The tanks also come equipped with laser wire-guided rockets. Unlike World War II vintage tanks, the M-1 model is swifter than some autos—traveling a brisk forty miles per hour over broken terrain—and can fire while it is on the move. The M-1 tank is a technological marvel, an instrument of war that has total vision even at night and uses computer-aided calculations to aim its weapons.

INCREDIBLE NEW ELECTRONIC WEAPONS

In any war in Europe or the Middle East, U.S. forces would be the numerical underdogs. Soviet forces hold the upper hand in terms of numbers of troops, tactical aircraft, tanks, and armored vehicles. Under these circumstances, U.S. strategy would have to compensate with superior weapons fortified with better technology that can properly be called "the great equalizers."

However, the Soviets are not sitting still. Their entire economy continues on a war footing and, with technology bought or stolen from the West, the Soviets would undoubtedly be able to field an armed force able to mount an enormous challenge.

Among new high-tech tools already in use or under development are the following:

- Sensors seeded behind enemy lines that will feed information on enemy formations and concentrations to distant U.S. Army computers.

- Optical cameras and vision equipment that allow armed forces to be able to see through darkness and fog.

- Airplanes that turn into helicopters and, by 1993, a new U.S. combat helicopter, the LHX, that will resemble the futuristic "Airwolf" and "Blue Thunder" choppers of TV and movie fame. The Soviets already have a deadly combat helicopter, the Mi-24 attack chopper, with air-to-ground missiles that can devastate a moving armored column on the ground below.

- Accurate and high-charged defense systems—ground weapons equipped with multiple rockets that release at hypervelocity speed.

- Tank-busting missiles such as the "Tank Breaker" being designed by Hughes Aircraft. This will be a one-man portable weapon using advanced optical sensors that see in darkness. The soldier fires his "smart" missile, which then autonomously seeks out the enemy tank.

Another missile system uses fiber optic cable which unspools as the missile speeds to its target. A soldier sits at a console and uses a TV screen to guide the missile to a direct hit. (The U.S. Army officer responsible for the operational evaluation of this system calls it "the ultimate video game.")

THE COMPUTERIZED BATTLEFIELD

Computers are going to war. The U.S. Army is adopting computers and computerized systems at a rate comparable to the civilian craze for home and personal computers. The army takes computers directly into battlefield action. One computer system, the DAZ3, operates inside an air-conditioned, thirty-five-foot-long trailer, and portable microcomputers have been installed aboard armored vehicles and jeeps.

The popularity of video games and home computers may have given the United States an advantage in the computerization of the military. President Reagan was quoted as telling a group of science and math students at Disney World's futuristic EPCOT Center that video games have helped young people develop "incredible hand, eye, and brain coordination." He added that computerized video screens resembled radar and electronic displays in jet cockpits, and he suggested that a game like Space Invaders will prove invaluable training to tomorrow's pilots.

Deputy Undersecretary of Defense Donald Latham says that by 1990 computers will have become an indispensable front-line necessity for the U.S. Army.

They will control communications systems to give commanders an unprecedented amount of information. In battlefield areas, ground computers will be on-line with aircraft and satellites to receive information about the enemy position and capability. With satellites providing communications links, front-line soldiers with hand-held and pocket computers will be able to communicate with distant units and with tanks and artillery. Computers will give commanders instant readouts on how battles are progressing and the status of reinforcements. They will also be programmed with artificial intelligence so they can advise battle staffs on the best courses of action. Fifth-generation computers that "think" may become battlefield strategists and decision-makers.[1]

The Soviet armed forces are lagging behind in the computer race, but recent developments suggest the Kremlin is giving high priority to computerizing the battlefield. Soviet spies now plague U.S. high-tech centers such as Silicon Valley in California and the metro areas of Boston, Austin, Orlando, Colorado Springs, and other areas where computer technology research is headquartered.

ROBOTS AND OTHER INTELLIGENT BATTLE MACHINES

Intelligent machines are causing a revolution in business and industry as computers and robots invade factory assembly lines and automated machines increasingly replace workers ranging from tellers in banks to longshoremen on loading docks. These machines are also being endowed with artificial intelligence to enable them to "see" and to exercise expert knowledge. The intelligent machine revolution has now spread to the military.

Just as robots work side by side with workers on General Motors, Chrysler, and Toyota assembly lines, the armed services are beginning to "recruit" robots and other intelligent machines to serve alongside human counterparts and to replace valuable biological combatants in dangerous tasks. Many of the new systems are already in use, though most are either in prototype stage or being researched. Included are remotely piloted aircraft for spy missions; flight simulators with incredible graphics displays; tracked robot vehicles that dismantle mines, bombs, and explosives; robot machines that load artillery weapons; robot scouts; and powerful multilegged walking robots that can maneuver easily and handle extremely heavy loads. In one official U.S. Army report, one hundred different robots were proposed for land warfare. The March 1983 issue of *Army Environmental Sciences* reported, "These types of intelligent machines will reduce the requirement to place soldiers in potentially high-risk combat environments."

Frank Verderame, assistant director of the army's research programs, says that an unmanned robot tank now under development, the tactical robot vehicle, "will be fitted with firepower so it can lead an assault." Operated by remote computerized control, he adds, such a vehicle will "be useful in traveling through areas contaminated by nuclear warfare or biological warfare."[2]

SRI International, commissioned by the U.S. government to study combat robots, emphasizes that the

Soviet Union is also developing military robots:
"USSR military artificial intelligence robotics capability will eventually constitute a threat to U.S. forces . . .
the Soviet Union is currently and will in the future,
pursue . . . robotics for the military."[3]

RIGHT OUT OF *STAR WARS*

Many weapons systems now on drawing boards, being
tested, or—in some instances—already in inventories
are dramatically different from any system in the annals of warfare. Akin to weapons envisioned by yesterday's science fiction writers, these weapons will make
tomorrow's battles an appalling panorama of terror.

Perhaps the most awe-inspiring of the new weapons
is the U.S. Army's tactical combat laser weapon. Previously designated "C-CLAW," but now continued under "Stingray" and other classified code names, this
weapon gives U.S. ground forces the capability to permanently damage the optic nerves of opposing forces
who look into laser light as it sweeps across the battlefield as much as five miles away. Other laser devices
will be used to disrupt and incapacitate enemy guid-
ance and weapons systems.

The Soviet Union is possibly ahead of the U.S. in
developing laser weapons. Intelligence reports indicate
the Soviets are ready to mass-produce laser and other
directed-energy weapons. These reports describe
ground-based Soviet weapons that have demonstrated
the capability to penetrate heavy armor, clear mines,
and obliterate tanks and people.

In a recent issue of *High Technology* magazine (May
1985), David C. Morrison, a senior research analyst at
the Center for Defense Information in Washington, out-

lined some of the laser and other electronic weapons systems. He included in his remarks a poignant, first-hand account—first reported in *Laser Focus* magazine—of what a harrowing psychological and physical experience such weapons will be for soldiers in the field. The account was by laser physicist C. David Decker, who sustained permanent eye damage in 1977 while working in the laboratory with a low-power laser.

"When the beam struck my eye I heard a distinct popping sound, caused by a laser-induced explosion at the back of my eyeball," said Decker. "My vision was obscured almost immediately by streams of blood floating . . ."

"The most immediate response after such an accident is horror," concluded Decker. "As a Vietnam War veteran, I have seen several terrible scenes of human carnage, but none affected me more than viewing the world through my blood-filled eyeball."

THE BIOELECTRONICS FACTOR

Lasers aren't the only weapons that offer attackers promise due to their lightning-fast, silent deadliness. The Soviet Union seems to be the leader in developing new radio frequency weapons designed to scramble an enemy's brain waves. According to the Defense Intelligence Agency, the Soviets have also perfected short-range, microwave technology devices that can "cook soldiers like a microwave oven." These beam weapons hit the individual without warning. The Soviets call them "bioelectronic weapons." Expect the new devices to be in the hands of Soviet troops by the mid-1990s.[4]

Doubters might recall that the U.S. embassy in Moscow was for years the victim of microwave attacks by

Soviet agents operating in nearby buildings. After three former ambassadors contracted cancer, the State Department was compelled by embassy employees to declare Moscow an unhealthy work post and provide 20 percent salary increases as hazardous work compensation.

U.S. Intelligence sources evidently know what the Soviet's microwave beams were intended to do, but they aren't telling. Since 1983, after protests by the White House, the microwave invasions have abated.

NEPTUNE'S ARSENAL

There will be no safety above or beneath the seas in coming years. Today's submarines and combat ships possess formidable power. America's *Trident* submarine carries 192 nuclear-tipped missiles, on eight platforms, with a range of 4,400 miles. (The Soviet's *Typhoon* sub has on board 200 missiles with a range of 6,000 miles.) Combat ships are equipped with Tomahawk cruise missiles, computerized guns, and electronic warfare systems. Aircraft carriers accommodate over seventy-five aircraft, each capable of being armed with nuclear bombs.

It's getting impossible to hide no matter how far beneath the seas a submarine plunges. New laser and satellite sensors scan deep beneath the seas and target submarines for destruction by nuclear depth charges and other means. Surface vessels are even more vulnerable. For example, two strategic air command B-52G squadrons will soon carry the new Navy Harpoon warhead missile, capable of seeking out an enemy warship sixty miles away and sinking it.

Among the sea weapons the United States possesses

is the F-14 Tomcat fighter aircraft. Beyond the range of enemy fighter radar, the sleek F-14 can track and evaluate up to twenty-four targets at once. Then, from a stand-off position as much as one hundred miles away, it can launch its six Phoenix missiles against the greatest threats—and still monitor the other eighteen targets.

Another effective war system is the USS *Ticonderoga,* a guided missile cruiser equipped with the computerized Aegis defense system. The Aegis robotic system automatically tracks hundreds of attacking aircraft or missiles, then fires and guides the ship's own weapons in response.

The USSR now has over 300 submarines; the U.S. has only 126. One Soviet submarine type is made of lightweight titanium, which makes it the fastest in the world. The Soviet subs operate in seas and waterways that once were solely U.S. "territory." Increasingly, they're spotted in the seas of Norway and Sweden, where they have ready access to the North Atlantic so that in wartime they could intercept U.S. convoys bound for Europe.

Submarines aren't the only staple of the Soviet ocean-going military force. Defense Department figures reveal that the Soviet navy has two helicopter carriers (the U.S. and the West have no equal) and 277 destroyers and frigates (compared to the West's 187). The Soviets have a total of 1,504 battle-ready, sea-based helicopters and aircraft while the West has only 1,129. The Soviet navy has in recent years intensified its efforts to build and deploy aggressively oriented amphibious attack vessels. One new Soviet amphibious assault ship is capable of carrying an entire infantry battalion with all its supporting vehicles.

Long considered a second-rate naval power, Moscow decided decades ago to build the world's mightiest sea force. Now, in the late 1980s, we are viewing the fruits of that massive, ongoing buildup.

The Soviets are not counting on just the hardware of war to make them superior—and neither is the U.S. In the next chapter we will examine some weapons that are almost unthinkable—weapons that operate through the power of the human mind *and* against the mind of the enemy. It should come as no surprise that man apart from God would not only wage war against property and physical life, but against the human mind as well.

ELEVEN
BRAIN INVADERS: PSYCHIC WARFARE

"There are weapons systems that operate on the power of the mind and whose lethal capacity has already been demonstrated." These were the words of U.S. Army Lt. Col. John B. Alexander in his startling article published by the U.S. Army's *Military Review Journal* in December 1980. In the article, Alexander discussed "psychotronic weapons" such as the use of telepathic hypnosis. He asserted: "The ability to heal or cause disease can be transmitted over distance, thus inducing illness or death for no apparent cause."

For those of you who are prone to believe that Lt. Col. Alexander possibly has lost his mind, consider the fact that this was an article published in a staid, conservative U.S. military journal read almost exclusively by senior military brass and civilian defense analysts. Actually, Alexander was merely summarizing some of the shocking conclusions already made by the Pentagon based on decades of ultrasecret research on mind control and psychic means of conducting warfare and intelligence operations.

At least three books discussing these topics have been recently published. There is the 1983 book *Psychic Warfare: Threat or Illusion?* by Martin Ebon, and 1984's *Mind Wars* by Ronald McRae. McRae's book centers on the research done by U.S. intelligence and military agencies. A third book, *The Mind Race* by Russell Targ and Keith Harary, also partially reviews U.S. efforts, but it is particularly enlightening in its examination of the Soviet drive to develop mind warfare. Targ, a physicist at SRI International, a California think tank, conducted psychic studies under contract with the U.S. Navy in the 1970s.

MIND WEAPONS: WHAT THEY ARE

There are a number of different mind control and psychic warfare techniques being studied. These include:

- Remote viewing—the ability of psychic personnel to read the contents of documents at a distance or to visualize the geographic layout of an enemy's distant military installation, or to discern troop, ship, or submarine whereabouts.
- Telepathic hypnosis—the use of mind power to command, at long distance, an enemy to do something he would otherwise not do. For example, order troops into an ambush or order an intelligence officer to divulge secret information to a planted spy.
- Disease projection—induce illness or death (especially heart attacks and asphyxiation)

from a distance. Uncontrollable fright and fear could also be generated by mind power.

- Mind alteration—the long-distance ability to cause an opponent's mind—say, that of a president or prime minister—to grow confused and unable to function.
- Psychokinesis—the moving of physical objects through mind power.

MIND WEAPONS: WHO HAS THEM?

It appears that the Soviet Union is far ahead in the mind race. In July 1985, columnist Jack Anderson revealed that information from classified CIA and Pentagon reports showed the Soviets are outspending the U.S. by at least 70 to 1 in mind war research. (Anderson called it "occult research," a most appropriate term in my opinion.)

The CIA's latest top-secret report estimates that it would take a budget of anywhere from $500 million to $1 billion for the United States to play catch-up. As it is, the U.S. is spending about $6 million each year for psychic research, the Soviets as much as $350 million.

Alarmed U.S. officials are taking the Soviet threat seriously. A 1972 Defense Intelligence Agency report, classified at the time as top-secret but declassified and released to the public in 1978, predicted that eventually the Soviets might be able to do some of the following:

A. Know the contents of top-secret U.S. documents, the deployment of our troops and ships, and the location and nature of our military installations.

B. Mold the thoughts of key U.S. military and civilian leaders at a distance.

C. Cause the instant death of any U.S. official at a distance.

D. Disable, at a distance, U.S. equipment of all types, including spacecraft.

In 1977, August Stern, a Soviet dissident residing in the West, told U.S. intelligence agents of Soviet work on "psychic energy" at a laboratory at Science City in Novosibirsk, Siberia. Stern revealed that sixty Soviet scientists were receiving unlimited funds to carry out their investigations. Russell Targ (*The Mind Race*), who met with Soviet scientists and discussed their work with them, observed that they were surprisingly open about their experiments. Targ says that their comments suggested that in the USSR the subjects of such research were forced to endure pain and cruelty. According to Targ, the Soviet scientists were evidently curious to know how American researchers carried out research *without* such brutal methods. They asked, "What do you do to keep your subjects from cracking up or going crazy during the experiments?"[1]

Laura Vilenskaya, a Soviet-trained engineer now living in California who participated in a number of Soviet experiences, described in *The Mind Race* some of the experiments that she knew about, some that she said were "inhumane." She confirmed that the Soviet Union has uncovered a number of psychically gifted persons able to perform uncanny tasks unaided by anything other than their minds. One woman was capable of psychokinetically moving small objects about at will. This same woman was able to induce burns on bystanders' skin and to completely stop an isolated frog's heart from beating. According to Vilenskaya, the professor in charge of this experiment, Gennady Sergeuev, explained later, "We found that [the frog's heart] was torn apart, as if bombarded by lightning balls of microscopic size. The energy flow can reach such incredible intensity."

Vilenskaya and other Soviet emigrés tell of a great number of research centers in the USSR devoted to psychic research for warfare. The Soviets are also increasingly examining the occult traditions of Eastern religions. The researchers believe that yoga and other Hindu disciplines may reveal methods that can be used to gain military advantage through mind control techniques.[2]

THE UNITED STATES EFFORT

The U.S. is concerned about the apparent Soviet successes. Although the Pentagon and service chiefs don't wish to be branded by the news media as advocating "witch doctors" or "voodoo magic," they have been able to discreetly funnel tens of millions of dollars into the battle to develop mental tools of war. Up to now, the U.S. effort has met with only limited success. However, in a few instances, the success has been significant enough to influence Congress to continue funding such projects. One successful project was SRI International's long distance remote-viewing experiments, sponsored by the U.S. Navy. In the experiments, persons with psychic skills were remarkably accurate in describing buildings and objects at geographically remote sites.[3]

In an interview in *Omni* magazine (July 1979), Congressman Charles Rose, chairman of the House Sub-committee on Intelligence, said of the SRI study: "What these persons saw was confirmed by aerial photography. . . . It seems to me that it would be a hell of a cheap radar system. And if the Russians have it and we don't we are in serious trouble."

Based on the SRI study as well as other experimentation, in 1981 the Committee on Science and Technology of the U.S. House of Representatives reported:

> Experiments on mind to mind interconnectedness have yielded some encouraging results. . . . Given the potentially powerful and far-reaching implications of knowledge in this field, and given that the Soviet Union is widely acknowledged to be supporting such research at a far higher and more official level, Congress may wish to undertake a serious assessment of research in this country.[4]

MIND WEAPONS: THE CHRISTIAN PERSPECTIVE

From a Christian perspective, it might be assumed that psychic and mind power abilities being demonstrated in labs run by the Soviets or other nations are of Satan. It could well be that Satan seeks to convince the world that such feats are not exclusively the province of God but instead are natural, controllable, scientific phenomena.

Psychic "spying" for use in intelligence work is a jarring notion. But even more jarring are mind alteration and telepathic hypnosis. Christians should tremble at the prospect of any government—even our own—being able to affect a person's mental state from a long distance. We are already painfully aware of the mental abuse of many persons, including many Christians, in the Soviet Union, persons whose minds have become so confused by drugs and chemicals that the state declares them insane and has them incarcerated. That mental disturbance could be accomplished without drugs—and at a considerable distance—is terrifying. Such tactics show a total lack of respect for human worth and a brutal disregard for the mind of man, made in God's image.

Humanity teeters on the very edge of the demonic when it not only brings into war tools that damage bodies and property but tools that can wreck the human mind. Torturers and masters of war have, through the ages, shown their inventiveness in causing agonizing physical pain, but the mind has been largely untouchable. That is no longer necessarily true. Now, even without the use of drugs or chemicals, man may have the power to carefully manipulate and possibly destroy the mind.

This should not surprise us. In a world beset with war fever, men will use any weapons available. In part III we will look at just how pervasive this war fever is.

PART THREE
War Fever

TWELVE
THE WORLD POWDER KEG: WHY WAR PREVAILS

The Center for Defense Information, a Washington, D.C., think tank that keeps a box score on the wars, rebellions, and violent uprisings that plague our modern world, tells us that war is on the rise. In the last three years alone, says the center, over 4 million people have been engaged in combat, with 45 of the world's 164 nations involved. The number of people killed? An estimated one to five million. Citing these gruesome statistics, political columnist James Reston commented, "They remind us of the madness and cost of violence in a world where half the human race is going to bed hungry every night." Reston firmly states that "the causes of war need debating."

He's right. We do need to debate the issue. The key question is, *Why do we have wars?*

The human behavior experts and the philosophers offer a variety of reasons for war and violence. Benedict Spinoza believed that basic human passions lay at the roots of conflict. Sigmund Freud believed that conflicts were inevitably resolved by violence due to man's psychological makeup. Konrad Lorenz theorized that humans have inherent aggressive instincts just as do other animals.

Karl Marx, father of communism, believed that man himself is good, but that the economic structures of society cause him to make war and create violence. Social welfarists agree. They feel that if only the economic rewards of society were more equally distributed to the poor and deprived, violence would abate. Many political scientists hold that war is inevitable because we do not have a supranational body—a "supergovernment" capable of enforcing order. Create such an all-powerful center of government, they claim, and wars will cease. Unfortunately, the minds of men have not been able to conceive of a one-world supergovernment that works. Both the 1920s' League of Nations and today's United Nations have proved dismal failures.

Peace has been unattainable in our generation—as in all generations—primarily because men are not willing to share, to love, and to put aside selfish motives and the desire for personal gain. Furthermore, man cannot develop these caring and beneficial attitudes when left to his own devices. Man is a being torn between Satan and God. He must choose to serve one or the other. If he denies God, the inevitable result is a clouded, imperfect, and potentially dangerous perception of the world and the way things should be. War is a natural, unavoidable outgrowth of man's rejection of God.

James was inspired by the Lord to explain the causes

of war. In the New Testament, James explained it this way:

> From whence come wars and fightings among you? Come they not hence, even of your lusts that war in your members? Ye lust and have not: ye kill, and desire to have, and cannot obtain: ye fight and war, yet ye have not. . . . (James 4:1, 2)

According to the Bible, war is caused by selfish, ungodly men who lust after what they do not have and willingly kill to attain the objects of their desires. The answer to war would be for man to accept the spiritual riches that come from commitment to Christ. The Christian, the man of God, does not start wars nor commit violence in a vain and angry quest for material possessions that are of this world. For as Paul reminds us, "God hath not appointed us to wrath, but to obtain salvation by our Lord Jesus Christ" (1 Thess. 5:9). But evil seems to dominate the world scene because so many are not committed to life in Christ.

THE REALITY OF EVIL

On an international scale man's selfish attitude reflects itself in envy, greed, hatred and, eventually, conflict. Modern warfare, in its savagery and lethality, is unparalleled in the annals of history. Already this century we have seen hundreds of wars and millions of casualties. World Wars I and II brought untold misery to mankind. Since 1945—the year World War II ended—warfare has been experienced in Southeast Asia, Africa, Central and South America, the Middle East, and Eastern Europe. And terrorism has reared its head in almost every city on the globe.

Terrorism and conflict between nations is something that most people in America, the West, and other civilized democratic countries cannot fully grasp. War and killing, we tend to believe, are alien to our way of life and to our ways of thinking. But the truth which many seek to avoid is that every one of us is susceptible to evil if we exclude God and his Holy Spirit from our hearts. Within the darkness of every unenlightened human heart is the capability to have been a cruel guard at Dachau, a murderer on death row, or a terrorist who indiscriminately slays women and children. If God is absent from our lives, the only difference between us and "them" is circumstances. "There, but for the grace of God, go I."

Over 50 million people perished in the World War II holocaust, in which unspeakable acts occurred with official government sanction. Some protest that such evil could not happen again. They say we are too educated today, too knowledgeable, too enlightened, too humanitarian. Many teachers, especially those involved with the New Age movement, profess belief in a modern world where goodness and peace are winning out because man's consciousness is ever-expanding. In truth, the opposite is the case. Each year, corrupt and heartless authoritarian and totalitarian dictatorships in dozens of nations perpetrate grotesque acts of terror and violence against their own citizenry. Mass arrests, brutal torture, confinement without trial, and political suppression are the rule rather than the exception as we move toward the last days.

Reports from respected journalists and reliable witnesses indicate that the world is becoming a den for sadistic, incredibly cruel masters. Last year, for example, at Evin prison in Iran, children were forced to watch as their mothers were tortured. In Syria police employ the "black slave," an electrical apparatus with a heated skewer, and in Chile military interrogators are skilled in applying methods such as the "parrot's perch," in which a trussed prisoner is hung upside down from a pole and brutalized. In Guatemala during 1978-82, government dissidents were routinely burned with cigarettes, castrated, slashed, or suffered amputations. In the Soviet Union, prisoners continue to live in gulags, remote, rat-infested prison camps where the daily gruel is served with roaches and rat fecal material floating on top.

There are over 160 nations on earth, less than 30 of which are true democracies. Furthermore, citizens of America, Britain, Australia, Canada, and other democratic countries hardly understand the desperate nature of most of the earth's population. Noted science author Nigel Calder, in his recent book *1984 and Beyond,* made this keen observation:

> Our cosy liberal democracies now seem like small rafts of reasonableness on an ocean of irrationality, injustice, and terror. . . . They look more like happy accidents, extremely rare in history, and confined to a few parts of the globe. [1]

MODERN MARTYRS, MODERN HITLERS

"In the past 65 years, more Christians have given their lives in witness to Christ than in the 300 years which followed the crucifixion," wrote Mary Craig in her moving book *Six Modern Martyrs*. "Not even the gladiators and wild beasts of Decius and Diocletian have matched in ferocity the tidal waves of hatred unleashed in our century."[2]

Across the planet, unknown martyrs are giving their lives for Christ. Many languish and eventually perish in communist prisons in the Soviet Union, Poland, Vietnam, North Korea, and elsewhere. Others become the victims of authoritarian Marxist dictators in such countries as Ethiopia, Nicaragua, and Cuba.

There is no dearth of modern-day martyrs—or modern-day Hitlers. A review of only a few recent mass murderers shocks us into understanding the real and present danger confronting us today.

Uganda and Amin. In the 1970s, Ugandan dictator Idi Amin, an admirer of Hitler's treatment of Jews, put to death hundreds of thousands of his fellow Ugandans. Rape, torture, and brutalization were rampant. Reportedly, the eyes of some who fought the dictatorship were gouged out, and other dissidents were killed and their bodies fed to crocodiles. Shocking though it may seem, many nations in the Arab world and in the United Nations supported Amin.

As perverse as Amin's reign was (he was overthrown in 1979), it pales in comparison with the gory example set a few years ago by the leader of another Third World nation—Cambodia.

Cambodia and Pol Pot. In April 1975, the Communist Khmer Rouge led by Pol Pot seized power in the Southeast Asian nation of Cambodia. For centuries this small country had been known as the land of the gentle people, an oasis of tranquility and peace in Asia. The Khmer Rouge ended that. Their disturbing reign of terror began the day they gained control of the government. Pol Pot, their leader, announced his intention to "cleanse" the country.

By the time Pol Pot was overthrown four years later in 1979 after a war with neighboring Vietnam, his regime had seen to the massacre of over 3.5 million of Cambodia's total population of 7 million. (That's one-half of the population slain—the equivalent of 115 million persons in America!) To spare bullets, mass graves were dug and men, women, and children bludgeoned with tree limbs, clubs, and baseball bats. Among the first ordained to be murdered were those with an education. Even a high school diploma guaranteed an individual unmerciful torture and death.

Cities were seen as breeding places of intellectual dissent and hard-to-control mobs, so every major city in Cambodia was closed. All the residents were force-marched to the countryside. Without shelter, medicine, or food, most died. Torture became the commonly accepted practice of government officials, and atrocities became commonplace.

Hundreds of thousands of Cambodians sought refuge in neighboring Thailand, where even today they reside in squalid camps dependent on economic handouts from the United States. They are the lucky ones.

The tragic events in Cambodia were verified by scores of eyewitnesses and reported in major newspapers around the world.[3] In April 1978 President Jimmy Carter denounced Cambodia as "the worst violator of human rights in the world today."

Abduction, Torture, and Death in Argentina. The communists do not have a monopoly on terror. In Argentina in 1976, a right-wing military dictatorship rounded up over ten thousand men, women, and children. They were never heard from again. When mothers asked what had become of their children, authorities told them, "Forget you ever had a child . . . go home." It was not until 1983, after the military junta was replaced by civilian leaders, that parents learned of the fate of these ten thousand who were called the "disappeared." Many had been tortured to death. Some were forced into helicopters and taken aloft, then pushed out the door as the helicopters hovered over choppy seas. Other "disappeared" persons were summarily shot by firing squads and their bodies secretly buried in mass graves.

Imprisoning the innocent, bludgeoning guiltless men, women, and children to death, butchery on a mass scale—what drives a leader to order such heinous acts? Simply stated, it would be foolish to deny that such a leader is led by the forces of Satan. Alexander Solzhenitsyn, the exiled Russian author now living in the United States, stated recently that these horrible things happen when man is deprived of the divine dimension. "Men have forgotten God," said Solzhenitsyn. The absence of God from man's souls, he explained, has been "a determining factor in all the major crimes of this century."[4]

Devoid of God and the instinct for human kindness and compassion that the Holy Spirit brings to man, the shattering examples of twentieth-century leaders like Hitler, Amin, and Pol Pot and the atrocities occurring with regularity today around the globe jolt us to consider the reality of Satan and the darkness of his power.

WARS AND RUMORS OF WAR

The extreme cases of men like Idi Amin and Pol Pot should not mislead us into thinking that their appalling regimes were the exception to the rule. Terrorist activity anywhere in the world can at any moment shatter our confidence in the seeming impenetrability of our everyday, peaceful existence. More important, we must not become complacent in believing—erroneously—that major wars have become a thing of the past, exceptional occurrences that happen "over there" to "other people."

A reading of modern history reveals that since World War II over 10 million people have died in wars between nations. These casualties were inflicted by use of conventional (non-nuclear) weapons. However, the advent of nuclear weapons has fundamentally changed the nature of war. Ten million dead is a tiny number when compared to the number of deaths now possible if major war erupts. While there have always been wars and rumors of war, today the situation is unarguably different. Man gets more and more proficient in the profession of killing as time proceeds. Will Rogers once said, "Mankind is making progress. With every war he finds new ways to kill." The acquisition of nuclear weapons and other technological tools mean that, for the first time in history, man now has the capacity to physically destroy himself—erase all traces of civilization.

As the previous chapters illustrated, a future war will

see not only the explosion of great numbers of atomic weapons, but the employment of other weapons equally terrible and lethal: poisonous chemical and biological agents, people-killing neutron bombs, deadly laser rays, and even mind weapons. We are today seeing an unparalleled revolution in the development of weapons of war that is bringing us frighteningly close to Armageddon.

A look at the hazards of science and technology causes many to wonder if man has much longer to live on our planet. Millions demonstrate in the cities of the world in favor of a nuclear arms freeze. They fear the universe will go up in flames, destroyed by the blast of atomic weapons and the deadly radiation that swiftly follows.

THE PROPHETS AND THE EXPERTS

No shortage of experts warn us that unless man's attitude changes, advances in science and technology will eventually lead man to the ultimate disaster. The prophets of the Old and New Testaments prophesied that the final climax of man's reign on earth will occur as a culmination of world war. The Book of Revelation paints a picture of a brutal end as war envelops the planet. And Jeremiah also prophesied widespread slaughter:

> And the slain of the earth shall be at that day from one end of the earth even unto the other end of the earth: they shall not be lamented, neither gathered, nor buried; they shall be dung upon the ground. (Jer. 25:33)

Since the invention of nuclear weaponry some forty years ago, the voices of scientists have seemed to echo the warnings of the biblical prophets. Albert Einstein once warned, "There is no defense in science against the weapons which can destroy civilization." Reinforcing Einstein's comments, Dr. W. H. Pickering of the Air Force's Jet Propulsion Laboratory has stated that "in half an hour, the East and West could destroy civilization." And President Dwight D. Eisenhower chillingly observed, "Science seems ready to confer upon us, as its final gift, the power to erase human life from this planet."

The nightmarish prophecies of Revelation are clearly in the recesses of many experts' minds. William Koenig (*The Weapons of World War III*) recognized the biblical parallel when he stated, "Atomic weapons provide modern Western man with his vision of Apocalypse in the form of a nuclear holocaust."[5]

In a reference to the incredible progress in weapons technology, U.S. Air Force Lt. Col. John F. Guilmartin, Jr., editor of *Air University Review,* remarked in an editorial in that journal, "The marvels of science and technology push the realities of war far beyond the experience of ordinary life to rival in stark reality the symbolic horrors of the Apocalypse."[6]

The worldwide spread of weapons is evidence of the wisdom and vision of the prophet Joel, who foresaw the day when the posession of armaments would become a worldwide obsession: "Beat your plowshares into swords, and your pruninghooks into spears; let the weak say, I am strong" (Joel 3:10).

Strangely, no one seems to be in favor of armaments

and conflict. From the public expressions of world leaders, peace is a precious commodity. The very word *war* is an outdated anachronism. The Soviet Union describes itself as a "peace-loving country," and the United Nations Charter decries war and aggression. Common citizens are banding together in the quest for peace and many march and demonstrate to protest the nuclear build-up and to demand disarmament. Military analyst and author James Dunnigan (*How to Make War*) perhaps best expressed the sentiment of the average world resident when he said, "Real war is ugly, destructive, and remembered fondly only by those who survived it without getting too close."

THE WORLD AS AN ARMED CAMP

If all the world—or, at least, most of it—abhors war, one might wonder why the world has now become an armed camp. Not only the two superpowers are arming themselves to the teeth. Every nation on earth is preparing for war. Even the poorest countries empty out their treasuries to buy the newest military gadgets and devices. In these days, as Joel prophesied, even the weak gird themselves with tanks and bombs and proclaim, "I am strong."

Global military spending in 1985 reached $810 billion. Most of this was spent by the United States, the Soviet Union, Red China, West Germany, France, and Great Britain. But countries such as Israel, Egypt, Saudi Arabia, Iran, Ethiopia, and Poland also spent huge amounts for arms. In fact, according to the U.S. Arms Control and Disarmament Agency, smaller countries like Pakistan, Cuba, Libya, Czechoslovakia, Kuwait, and Singapore spent a far greater proportion of their national wealth on armaments than did the United States. War fever is not exclusively a disease of America or Russia. In fact, a United Nations report found that in 1982 Third World countries spent six times more on arms than they did on public health.

Some warlike countries are so bent on war and bloodshed that they import mercenaries and warriors from foreign lands. Libya, for example, possesses an air force of over two hundred aircraft, but has had to bring in pilots from North Korea, Syria, Pakistan, and other countries to fly its aircraft.

In the last twenty-five years, though millions of desperate people in poverty-stricken lands died due to starvation and lack of medical treatment, the combined military budgets of the world's nations increased a staggering 700 percent.

THE TWO GIANTS MAKE READY

Though many nations now devote enormous chunks of their budgets to military spending, the U.S. and USSR have the most to spend, and their arsenals dwarf all others. Both nations are on an arms binge. The United States has increased its military budget about 50 percent over the past five years. However, most of this was spent in an attempt merely to catch up to the Soviets who, during the 1970s, lavished a steady 12 to 14 percent of their gross national product on the military sector. The Soviets continue to spew out tanks, submarines, infantry weapons, and combat ships at an unbelievable pace, and Washington is running a huge budget deficit as it pumps up spending to insure a military equivalence with Moscow.

Regardless, U.S. defense experts report the USSR is

far ahead in many military categories, and the Soviets both outgun and outman the U.S. in such vital areas of the world as the Middle East and Europe.

Why do the Soviets dig so deeply into their pockets to build rockets and other armaments? Evidently, the masters in the Kremlin have a grand strategy yet to be revealed. They cry "Peace!" and condemn the U.S. and Europe, claiming we are preparing for—and thirst for—war; but in reality they are pulling out all stops to equip the world's mightiest striking force. With impressive propaganda, the Kremlin fools millions around the planet into believing that their nation is peace-loving and will never be the first to attack. However, the Russians' actions clearly reveal the corrupt plans of the Soviet Union. The whole Communist apparatus, the evidence demonstrates, is gearing for major war.

Also preparing for war are China, Japan, and East and West Germany. China has been on a war footing since the Communists took control of Peking in 1949, while Japan and both Germanys are devoting more national resources to defense than ever before. Defeated in World War II, these Asian and European powers are destined to play a large role in the military and political events leading up to the climactic furor of Armageddon.

LIGHTING THE FUSE

Who can deny that the planet is today a powder keg? Fearful anticipation grips people everywhere as they survey the world and envision a coming hour in which missiles and strategic bombers are unleashed and streak across the skies toward their targets. The winds of war rustle past us each day, and the entire world has become hostage to an overpowering, malevolent force greater than all of us.

All that's necessary to ignite the powder keg is the lighting of the fuse. In succeeding chapters, I'll examine those areas of the world where the fuse that leads to World War III might be lit.

THIRTEEN
FLASHPOINT: THE MIDDLE EAST

On April 18, 1983, an explosion rocked the U.S. Embassy in Beirut, Lebanon. Sixty-three people perished, foreshadowing a grim event yet to come. Some six months later, on a Sunday morning, October 23, a suicide driver smashed a truck loaded with explosives into a barracks housing United States Marines. The deafening roar was followed by the moaning of the wounded and the plaintive cries of the survivors mourning their slain companions. The death toll was 241 U.S. Marines.

These events in a faraway biblical land wracked by violence and treachery brought home to Americans and, indeed, the world a vital and ominous truth: the crises in the Middle East will just not go away. Instead, scores of nations around the world are in danger of being sucked into the swirling vortex of the politics of this region. Chief among them: the United States and the Soviet Union.

AN ABUNDANCE OF HATRED AND TURMOIL

Animosities and strife are rampant throughout the region. The hostility between Jews and Muslims is widely known, and many Muslims are also hostile toward Israel's allies, including the U.S. According to the *Times* of London, one prominent Muslim leader, Hussein Mussavi, head of the Shi'ite Muslim Party of God, said of the October 1983 massacre of U.S. Marines: "I personally consider this deed is a good deed which God loves and which his prophet [Muhammad]—may God praise his name—loves. I bow to the souls of the martyrs who carried out this operation."

At any time the entire Middle East region could go up in flames. Danger lurks within and without. Russian army divisions wait just across the northern borders of Iran and Turkey, while pro-Soviet regimes in Libya, Ethiopia, and South Yemen present threats on the southern borders. A Soviet armada of ships and submarines patrols the waterways adjacent to the Middle East landmass, flanked by the might of the United States fleet.

From within, we see hatred and venom between rival Muslim religious groups. The Holy Mosque in Mecca, Saudi Arabia, was the scene of a violent dispute between a rabid, radical group and government forces; dozens were killed. Iran's dominant Shi'ite Muslim group is known to be spreading terrorism across the region as it carries on an Islamic holy war espoused by leader Ayatollah Khomeini. In Iran itself, the Shi'ites, led by the clergy, continue to torture and execute those who are not of the officially sanctioned faith and political ideology.

Sources say that more inhumane acts have been committed by the present Teheran government in a few short years than during decades of rule under the late, deposed shah, himself accused by the Muslim clerics of brutality. Thirty thousand persons have been put to death since 1981, and testimony exists of grisly torture, including "ironing rooms" in Teheran's Evin prison in which victims are tied to a bed while guards burn their backs, buttocks, and the soles of their feet with a searing hot iron.

Turmoil is everywhere. In nearby Turkey, martial law has been imposed by army officers who took control in 1980. In Greece, an elected premier criticizes the United States, praises socialism, and threatens to pull out of NATO. Libya is led by Muammar Qaddafi, called a madman by the late Egyptian President Anwar Sadat, himself assassinated a few years ago. Iran and Iraq remain locked in a war that has seen hundreds of thousands of victims, including many who died and suffered horrible injuries due to chemical attacks by the Iraqi armed forces. And the Palestine Liberation Organization continues to lurk in the Middle East.

The impoverished and abused people of this region are extremely unhappy with their despotic leaders. In 1980, the CIA reported that of the regimes of ten Middle Eastern countries the agency studied, not a single one had better than a 40 percent chance of surviving past 1990. The Koran, the holy book of Islam, calls for a just and equal society, yet the oil sheiks and princes live in luxury in palaces and drive in their Mercedes and Cadillacs, passing diseased children and starving beggars along the way. Many observers believe it only a matter of time until explosive, angry mobs led by self-appointed holy men overthrow the idle rich now in power in the capitals of the Middle East.

THE HOVERING STORM CLOUDS

At one time not so long ago, the Middle East was a placid and peaceful territory. Multinational oil companies of the United States controlled the sheiks who ruled the oil-rich lands of the Persian Gulf, and U.S. allies France and Britain exerted great influence in the region. The United States built Iran into a powerful military fighting force as a bulwark against the threat of Muslim insurrection and Russian intervention.

Then the U.S. empire began to unravel. Militant leaders came to power, blasting America for its aid to Israel. Saudi Arabia and other Persian Gulf states cut off oil supplies to the U.S. and the West to punish us for supporting Israel. The sheiks took command of their oil holdings from the corporations and jacked the price of the black gold to unheralded heights, throwing the economies of Europe, the United States, and Japan into turmoil.

Then in 1979 came the fall of America's friendly Iranian leader, the shah, and the takeover of Iran by radical Muslim clergy who hate Washington, D.C., and detest the Jews. The taking of U.S. hostages and the U.S. embassy in Teheran followed. These incredible events came on the heels of another ominous act. The Soviet Union sent commandos, tanks, and troops into Afghanistan, seizing the reigns of power in that country bordering oil-rich Iran. Suddenly, America's position in the Middle East seemed a precarious one.

While the Arabs look ultimately to America for protection against the Russians, our only true ally in the region is Israel. The *Jerusalem Post* reported in 1984 that "a radically new defense alliance" is being woven between the nations of Israel and the United States. Evidently, it is hoped that such a military alliance will scare off the Soviets. The reasoning by Washington is that the Russians may be deterred from invasion of Israel and the Persian Gulf because of possible retaliation by Israel's ally, the United States. However, there is no guarantee that this strategy will prevent superior Soviet armed forces from crashing across the borders of Israel and other countries in the Middle East.

AMERICA'S WEAKNESS EXPOSED

The White House well understands the weakness of this country's exposed position in the Middle East. In fact, there is little doubt that President Ronald Reagan and his military and political advisors worry constantly about the cauldron of this troubled region boiling over. Recently, in a conversation with Thomas Dine, executive director of the American-Israeli Public Affairs Committee, the president noted that he had talked the night before to parents of a Marine killed in Beirut. Then, he made this startling comment:

> You know, I turn back to your ancient prophets in the Old Testament and the signs foretelling Armageddon, and I find myself wondering if—if we're the generation that is going to see that come about. I don't know if you've noted any of these prophecies lately, but, believe me, they certainly describe the times we're going through. [1]

The president knows that the Middle East has the potential to explode at any time and that events there could catapult the United States and the Soviet Union into a worldwide nuclear war. So, too, do the Joint Chiefs of Staff at the Pentagon and almost every other military expert. In November 1980, in *Air Force* magazine, Gen. T. R. Milton, USAF (Ret.), stated, "The Mideast, after years of threatening to do so, is giving signs of coming apart. We are threatened in a way we have never been threatened before."

What General Milton was referring to was the shakiness of America's military posture in the Middle East. In the same article, Milton remarked: "The nearby presence of 27 divisions on the Iranian border makes our own corporal's guard of Marines floating around the Indian Ocean scarcely even a symbol of American resolve and power."

Since 1980, the military equation has changed little. The Soviet Union still has a preponderance of military force. As next-door neighbors, they are as close to the vital Persian Gulf oil region of the Middle East as the United States is to Toronto in Canada or Mexico City in Mexico. In 1982, the foreign affairs panelists at the National Security Conference authored a report which spoke of U.S. military capability in the Middle East: "Our current forces are big enough to get us into trouble, but not big enough to get us out . . . we simply cannot project any significant force into the region and sustain it there."

In June 1984, a report of the Defense Appropriations Committee of the House of Representatives detailed the weaknesses of the U.S. military. According to the report, this country's armed forces could not sustain themselves—could not win—in the event of a non-nuclear conflict in either Europe or the Middle East. This is ironic, for the U.S. defense budget is at an all-time high.

The Pentagon is building a formidable U.S. strategic fighting force comprised of thousands of nuclear bombs, impressive missilery, neutron bombs, space and laser weapons, and other advanced systems. But meanwhile, the *conventional* fighting capacity of our military—the traditional ground, sea, and air components—may not be sufficiently capable of fighting a Soviet armed force superior in numbers and conventional weapons.[2]

THE NUCLEAR OPTION

Under such circumstances, the only alternative an out-manned U.S. force might have is the atomic bomb option. In other words, faced with sure defeat, the danger is that the U.S. will face two harsh choices: surrender or nuclear war.

The Middle East lies within the geographic sphere of the Soviet Union, and the Kremlin continues to beef up its conventional forces based near the region. Sometime in the not too distant future, the president of the United States will be forced to choose between a nuclear holocaust and the bitterness of surrender.

Would the Soviet Union be so brash as to initiate a conflict that might result in a holocaust? In the 1973 Arab-Israeli war, as Israel's victorious tanks hemmed the Egyptian forces in a vise grip and were going in for the kill, the Kremlin sent this message to President

Nixon over the Moscow-to-Washington hotline: "Tell the Israelis to cease their attack or Soviet forces will enter the war on the side of Egypt."

Nixon knew the Kremlin's leader, Brezhnev, meant business, for U.S. intelligence agencies told Nixon that Soviet ships carrying atomic warheads had docked at Cairo. Since in essence the Israelis had already won the war, Nixon called on them to order a truce and stop fighting. Reluctantly, Israel complied.

PRETEXT FOR WAR

In the war that seems inevitable, the Soviet Union may once again use the outbreak of Arab-Israeli hostilities as a pretext to intervene. Other opportunities also present themselves. The Kremlin may itself, through its KGB and GRU secret intelligence agents, have a Soviet embassy in Iran, Saudi Arabia, or Israel sacked, then blame the local government and send in its troops as "retaliation." Another scenario may be that Soviet forces are sent in, uninvited, to "assist" a Middle East regime undergoing a rebellion by its unhappy citizenry. Or the Soviets may, totally unprovoked, send in their tanks and airplanes in a sneak attack.

THE RICHES OF ISRAEL AND THE MIDDLE EAST

The treasure available to the Soviet Union in the Middle East is fabulous beyond measure. The conquest of this region would be the greatest achievement ever for the Communist dictators in Moscow. Materially, its possession would put in their hands the world's largest oil reserves, plus the technological wealth of Israel, one of the most prosperous and economically developed nations on earth. It would provide the Russian navy a permanent and reliable warm water port. (By treaties and other arrangements, the Soviets have warm water bases in the Indian Ocean.) Most important of all, Soviet possession of the Middle East oil spigot would make Russia the undisputed economic czar of the entire world. The West and Japan would be brought to their knees and forced to crawl to the Kremlin begging for oil rations.

In his book *The Real War,* former President Richard Nixon revealed a statement that intelligence sources attributed to former Soviet Leader Leonid Brezhnev. Speaking before a closed meeting of Communist party chieftains, Brezhnev declared, "Our aim is to gain control of the two great treasure houses on which the West depends—the energy treasure house of the Persian Gulf and the mineral treasure house of central and southern Africa."[3]

The Lure of Oil. The Middle East is the Klondike of world oil. Saudi Arabia alone holds over one-fourth of the earth's oil reserves—167 billion barrels. Over 75 percent of Japan's energy is supplied by the Arab sheiks of Saudi Arabia and nearby countries such as Kuwait, Bahrain, Qatar, Oman, Abu Dhabi, Iraq, Iran, and the United Arab Emirates. The region also supplies two-thirds of European oil needs. Even though the United States acquires a much smaller portion of its oil from this region, past history and recent studies demonstrate how vulnerable is the United States to an oil cutoff in the Middle East. In 1983 the National Energy

Foundation reported that such a cutoff would produce domestic price rises of over 300 percent. Furthermore, the U.S. Department of Energy states that alternative energies will not be available until at least the year 2025, and that oil will be the mainstay for the U.S. economy through the year 2000.

As we will discuss in the following chapter, the Soviet Union has fallen on hard times. Its rigid economy is on the verge of collapse. What a transfusion the incredible oil reserves of the Middle East would provide the weakened and ailing Soviet giant! In one swift stroke, a Soviet invasion could ease the Soviet economic crisis while causing chaos to the economies of bitter foes America, Western Europe, and Japan.

Israel's High-Tech Prosperity. Another plum awaiting Soviet troops is the intellectual and economic affluence of modern-day Israel. One of the chief problems in Soviet Russia today is that country's backwardness in high technologies—computers, robotics, lasers, microelectronics, and others. Much of the Soviet military weaponry and technology consists of cheap imitations of U.S. and other foreign-built products. In Israel, world observers note a sensational high-technology boom. Similar to the growth of Silicon Valley in California, high-tech breakthroughs are becoming commonplace throughout Israel.

Few Americans and foreigners are aware of the breadth and scope of Israel's high-tech economy. But its world competitors—international corporations such as AT & T, IBM, Boeing, and Lockheed—*are*. Let's examine some of the spectacular efforts of Israel's scientists and technicians.[4]

Worldwide Corporate Leadership. In 1970, according to Israeli government sources, export sales of high-tech products by Israeli corporations accounted for a puny $8 million. By 1984 they had mushroomed to a staggering $1.3 billion. Among Israel's largest high-tech companies are Israel Aircraft Industries, Ltd. (jet aircraft and computer electronics), Iscar (jet engines), Elron (computers, electronics, and biotechnology), El-Op (lasers and communications), Tadinan (electronics and telecommunications), Ormat (solar technology), and Israel Chemicals (chemicals and pharmaceuticals).

All of these firms and many others are vigorous competitors in world markets. For example:

- Laser Industries, Ltd., of Tel Aviv, a pioneer in the fast-growing laser field, has captured some 60 percent of the world market for CO_2 medical lasers, increasingly used for precision surgery in hospitals and clinics around the globe.
- Elscint, a Haifa-based firm, specializes in computerized axial tomography scanners (CATSCAN), machines used in advanced medical diagnosis. The company has a large share of the world market, though it competes head-on with such powers as General Electric and Toshiba.
- Israel's chemical industry is growing at a rapid pace. One firm begun only a few years ago, Periclase Chemicals, exploits the mineral-rich Dead Sea. It earns more than $27 million annually from export of magnesium and hydrochloric acid products.
- The Israeli bioengineering industry is among

the world's leaders in this technology. The *Jerusalem Post* reported in March 1984 that over $100 million had been spent in the previous five years for biological research and development.

Impressive Internal Development. Internally, Israel is being transformed into a progressive, high-tech oasis. Here are three examples:

- Israel is plunging into space. It will launch its first telecommunications satellite in 1987, a $250 million project, and Israeli scientists have conducted experiments aboard America's space lab.
- Computers are being used on a massive scale to manage Israeli farms. Ehud Gol, Israel's consul in New York, says that his country's farmers now use computers to determine precise fertilization needs and to make tractors more efficient.
- Israel has begun a $1.3 billion hydroelectric system that will shift 1.6 billion cubic meters of water annually from the Mediterranean to the Dead Sea. Scheduled for completion by 1995, the project will provide Israel with vast amounts of electric power, reduce the salinity of the Dead Sea, and rejuvenate the lands that surround it.

Israel's Growing Military Power. In a few key areas, Israel's military technology rivals that of America's. On June 9, 1982, F-15 and F-16 fighter bombers of the

Israeli air force totally decimated Syria's Soviet-built antiaircraft batteries, tanks, and vehicles in Lebanon's Bekaa Valley. They also shot down eighty-six Soviet-built MIG aircraft but themselves suffered *no losses of aircraft*. These victories were attributed to advanced electronics systems designed by Israel's scientists and installed on their U.S.-built aircraft. American experts say that these technologies are superior to what U.S. laboratories have devised. Israel has also begun to build complete aircraft and even sells military parts and equipment to other countries. One military electronics company, AEL Israel, has increased exports 500 percent in recent years. AEL Israel employs a 500-member research staff.

When World War II ended, a victorious Soviet army kidnapped East German scientists and brought them to Russia, putting them to work developing weapons for the Soviet military. Entire factories and industrial plants were dismantled in the sectors of Germany occupied by Russian troops and shipped back home to Russia where they were reassembled and placed into production. No doubt the Soviets would treat Israeli scientists and industry in a similar fashion. The rapidly expanding laboratories and research institutes of Israel and the more than fifty thousand Israeli scientists and engineers would be a terrific bonanza for the Soviet Union. For Moscow, these are spoils for which bloodshed is a small price to pay.

GOD'S HAND

Israel's high-tech prosperity is especially a miraculous accomplishment in light of this country's bleak geography, small population (about 4 million), and lack of natural resources. As Michael Knipes of the *Times* of London has noted, "It is indeed striking that a country with the same population as Philadelphia should be capable of maintaining seven universities, an aerospace industry, its own Army, Navy, and Air Force, and compete with the world's leaders in technologies."

The mind-boggling high-tech developments in Israel should cause persons who refuse to believe in prophecy to pause and reflect. The Bible's prophecies accurately predicted that the people of Israel would be cast out from their country and scattered across the world. The prophecies stated that, though they would suffer as hostages in other countries, the children of Israel would, in the last days, be restored to their ancestral lands. Further, God's prophets clearly told us that the revived state of Israel would then prosper, so much that the "King of the North" (Russia) would one day be overcome with greed and invade Israel and its neighbors "to take a spoil" (Ezek. 38:10-12).

All this the prophets predicted—and every word has come true, proof that God's hands hold up our universe and that his will shall be done on earth.

AMERICAN PREPAREDNESS FOR WAR

Though at a geographic and military disadvantage, the United States will fight to prevent a Soviet victory in the Middle East. U.S. military leaders rightly perceive that any overt Soviet military action in the Middle East constitutes a threat to world order. Following the Russian thrust into Afghanistan, Army Chief of Staff Gen. E. C. Meyer stated flatly that "World War III started on December 27, 1979"—the date the Soviets invaded Afghanistan, right on the fringe of the volatile Middle East.[5]

President Jimmy Carter quickly stated the readiness of the United States to use force to protect the strategic oil resources of the Persian Gulf. In his January 1980 State of the Union Address, Carter warned the Soviets:

> Let our position be absolutely clear: An attempt by any outside force to gain control of the Persian Gulf region will be regarded as an assault on the vital interests of the United States of America, and such an assault will be repelled by any means necessary, including military force.[6]

Soon after Carter's speech, the Pentagon announced the creation of a Rapid Deployment Force, a trained and alert-ready contingent to be deployed to the Middle East on short notice in event of Soviet attack. Meanwhile, by early 1981, the bombers and crews of the U.S. Air Force's Strategic Air Command (SAC) were holding dress rehearsals for a future nuclear mission to the Middle East. Said Gen. Richard Ellis, commander of SAC, in a *Washington Post* interview, "Our chances of stopping the Soviets on the landmass are extremely limited." Ellis explained that if, say, the U.S. Marines were about to be slaughtered on the ground by overwhelming Soviet might, U.S. leaders would be forced to resort to nuclear weapons to prevent total defeat.

In the same article, Air Force pilot Maj. Jerry Swank, of Lucerne, Indiana, remarked, "We can get into an area very fast. . . . In two or three days we can be bombing."

Most Americans simply don't realize how close the world is to the precipice of war. Our Sixth Fleet sits in the Mediterranean, flanked by opposing Soviet naval forces. Our naval base in the Indian Ocean, Diego Garcia, is watched carefully by patrolling Soviet warships and submarines.

President Ronald Reagan has ordered our forces in this area to be beefed up even further and, like Carter before him, the president has also warned the Soviets that war will result if they choose to march on Iran or another Persian Gulf country.[7]

In response, Russia has placed nearly one hundred thousand troops inside Afghanistan and has strengthened its naval forces in the area. Thus both sides prepare for war.

FOURTEEN
THE SOVIET UNION: MILITARY GIANT, ECONOMIC DWARF

The latter-day actions of the USSR make perfect sense to historians. Russia is an empire that has been built on greed and conquest. Territorial imperialism has long been the very foundation for the Kingdom of the North. Time and again, ruthless Russian rulers have proven their willingness to take by force the lands and riches of those nations unfortunate enough to be geographically adjacent to this imperialistic giant. In the case of the Marxist Soviets, greed combines with will to create a dangerous ideological foundation.

There is yet another factor that stirs up the greed and imperialistic ambitions of Moscow. That factor involves the tremendous internal problems faced by the Kremlin. Chief among these problems is the stagnant Russian economy.

THE ECONOMIC FAILURE OF THE COMMUNIST REGIME

The Soviet Union is slowly falling apart economically and is subject to collapse. This was the finding of a CIA study prepared for CIA Director William Casey in the summer of 1984. The intelligence analysts reported that after sixty-seven years in power, during which Moscow lavished resources on its military machine, the Communists could not provide sufficient food nor adequate medical care to the people. "At last, history seems to be catching up with the world's last surviving empire," concluded the report.

Historians say that the combination of economic weakness and military strength invariably leads a nation to war. Such was the case of Germany when Hitler plunged the world into war, and such is now the case for the Soviet Union.

The USSR undeniably has the world's premier military force. Its conventional forces are unparalleled, and its strategic might is at least equal—many say *superior* —to that of the United States. Yet, this military might has been assembled only at the expense of the economy, which borders on disaster. The perilous state of the economy and other severe internal problems will undoubtedly be the catalysts that induce Russia to decide on war. The Soviets will likely plot to solve their nation's problems by seizing the incomparably rich assets of the lands that lie south of Russia: the Persian Gulf nations and the wealthy and technologically advanced state of Israel.

Most economists agree that the Soviet Union is potentially the richest nation on earth. This is a vast country of over 250 million people which occupies one-sixth of the earth's land surface, stretching across the continents of both Europe and Asia. The USSR has the world's largest cache of natural resources. Known reserves include over half the world's coal deposits, 45 percent of its manganese, 60 percent of its potassium, 25 percent of its phosphates, and as much as one-third of all the world's timberland.

Nevertheless, the Soviet economy is faltering and on the brink of disaster. Amidst a huge store of natural resources Soviet citizens are suffering great personal deprivation.

Soviet observers are well aware of the horrible problems that have surfaced in the Russian economy. Numerous articles in such prominent publications as the *New York Times, Harper's, Wall Street Journal,* and the *Washington Post* have discussed these problems, and several excellent books have been published recently, most notably *The USSR in Crisis* by Marshall Goldman, *The Crisis in the Soviet System* by David Rousset, and *Russia: Broken Idols, Solemn Dreams* by David Shipler. These experts say that the economy is so bad and future prospects so bleak that the Soviet people have lost all faith in communism.

The bankruptcy of the Soviet system is evident when one considers that Moscow and its puppet states were forced during the 1970s to borrow $80 billion dollars from Western banks in a bid to stay solvent. Today, per capita consumption in the USSR is only one-third of that in the United States. The gross national product is actually declining, and in the 1980s the Soviet people are undergoing the worst times since Stalin's death in 1953. This is a nation that once promised its people that, by this decade, their standard of living would be higher than that of Americans. Today, the Kremlin refrains from such boasts for the future. It—and its enslaved people—know the sad truth.

THE HUNGER PROBLEM

The failure of the Soviet leadership to solve the agricultural problem has been a particularly crushing blow to the Russian people. People can do without many consumer goods, especially "luxury" items like appliances and automobiles. But food is another matter. And in the Soviet Union today adequate food supplies are simply not available.

The inflexibility of a system in which the farmers work collectively for the state has played havoc with production levels. For most farmers, their only motivation is to get through with work as soon as possible each day. There is no incentive to produce because, on a collective farm, the state and not the individual farmer reaps benefits that accrue from diligent labor.

It is amazing but true that in the world depression years of 1934-38, the Soviet Union produced such a large agricultural surplus that it was able to *export* 5 percent of its grain harvest. (This is even more remarkable considering that in 1932-33 there was famine in the Ukraine.) Yet, in the 1980s, it is forced to import one-third of its grain from the West. This is an indication of how badly mismanaged is Soviet agriculture.

RUSSIA JOINS THE OIL BEGGARS

In addition to the utter failure of their agricultural program, the Soviets are faced with another problem: the end of an oil surplus. Until now the Soviet Union has imported only a small fraction of its oil from other nations. This has given the Soviet economy a great advantage over the Western economies. However, Russia's advantage is now ending. Its supplies of oil

are fast being depleted. Even now, the Soviet Union
seeks to purchase natural gas from Iran and receives
oil from Iraq in exchange for military arms and
equipment.[1]

The problem is not lack of oil but, rather, that the
huge Soviet oil reserves are in difficult-to-get-at loca-
tions. The "easy to get" oil in Russia has already been
extracted. In the future, oil can be produced only at
great cost, using modern extraction techniques. Engineering problems caused by the horrible climatic and
geographical conditions in northern Siberia, where the
new oil exists, are worse than those experienced in development of America's oil reserves in Alaska. Even if
conditions were better, the poor attitude of the Soviet
workers and the lack of drilling technology limit
production.

Oil industry sources say that in oil exploration it
takes the Soviet Union fourteen months to drill to
10,000 feet. American technology can accomplish this
in thirty-four days. Thus, the cost to produce one barrel of oil in the USSR nearly exceeds the value of the
oil produced!

The Soviets' building of the Yamal Pipeline reflects
their acute need for Western oil technology. This massive construction project will enable billions of cubic
meters of natural gas to be piped 3,600 miles from remote Siberia to the populated centers of Russia and
Western Europe. Predictably, the Russians did not have
the $10 to $15 billion required to build this pipeline,
which was to be the longest in the world, so they obtained financing from the countries of Western Europe.
In exchange, the USSR promised to supply West Ger-

many, France, and other European nations with gas upon completion of the project. The pipeline will not be completed until at least 1990. Even then, the new gas will barely make up for Russia's depleted oil reserves.

A steady chorus of voices warns that the oil shortage may tempt the Soviets to invade the Middle East's Persian Gulf region and thus acquire its vast energy supplies.

Secretary of Defense Caspar Weinberger has frequently spoken out on the volatile situation that confronts the Soviet Union. In a speech given March 4, 1981, and reported through the media, Weinberger asserted that "the Soviet Union will almost certainly become a net energy importer." The secretary warned that economic necessity is forcing the Soviets to seek access to the Persian Gulf region.[2]

A DISILLUSIONED PEOPLE

The broken promises and dreams of their leaders have left many Soviet citizens demoralized and disillusioned. A large number have turned to alcohol to drown their troubles. Vladimir Trenl, a Duke University economist, has stated that alcohol consumption in the Soviet Union has more than doubled since 1955. The Soviet authorities themselves are alarmed over the magnitude of the alcohol problem. One Soviet journal, *Young Communist,* estimated that half the entire work force goes to work each day either drunk or suffering from a hangover. Other reports indicate that alcohol poisoning kills about 39,800 Russians annually, as compared to 400 Americans. No wonder worker productivity is declining!

For many people, alcohol is the only way a person can blot out the harsh realities—and failed promises—of the Soviet regime.

The silent revolt of the masses is also manifested in other ways. Crime is on the upswing throughout the USSR. Soviet newspapers complain about the lack of public order and say that the police appear helpless to prevent lawlessness. In *Pravda* in 1984 a commentator stated that the government is pursuing a vigorous campaign in workplaces against "absenteeism, loafing, and late arrivals at work."

A growing number of Soviet citizens are simply deciding that life in Russia isn't worth living. Western experts say that the suicide rate in the Soviet Union is nearly five times as high as that in the United States. The Soviet government refuses to report the actual figures. However, the United Nations does have statistics for other Soviet bloc countries. These figures show that Communist nations Romania, Hungary, and East Germany have the highest suicide rates in the entire world. Communist atheism has not proved an answer for these depressed peoples of Russia and the countries it holds captive; they see only death as an answer.

THE STRENGTH OF THE SOVIET BEAR

History instructs us that a nation beset internally by political and economic problems is often tempted to divert its people's attention by embarking on a war against others. War is a uniting force that would engage the energies of all the Soviet peoples. Considering the military balance now existing, the Soviet bear will have a decided advantage in the one place experts believe war is most likely: the Middle East.

In his 1982 report to Congress on "The U.S. Military Posture," Gen. David Jones, chairman of the Joint Chiefs of Staff, cautioned that while the United States can take action in the Middle East, "We cannot guarantee the outcome." Jones also reported that even if the U.S. sprinted to improve its defense posture, "the Soviet advantage cannot be offset in a year or even a decade."[3] Other experts are more blunt: They say the U.S. cannot win a war in this region. I agree. For the foreseeable future, this is absolutely the wrong place for the U.S. to fight a war. Let's discuss the reasons why.

Lack of U.S. Manpower. The Soviet Union has seven airborne and twenty-nine ground divisions (7,000 to 13,000 men each) available for combat in the Middle East. That makes for a grand total of approximately 350,000 troops. The Rapid Deployment Force (RDF) of the United States has at most about 15,000 troops of its 82nd Airborne Division, the 18,000 men assigned to the 101st Airmobile Division, and two amphibious Marine divisions of nearly 20,000 each, a total of about 53,000. Advantage for Russia: about 7 to 1.

In addition, the Russians have over 800 combat aircraft in this region (versus 170 the U.S. has on aircraft carriers), and massive reinforcements are less than a thousand miles distant.

The Russians know they will need this huge advantage. The valiant soldiers, airmen, seamen, and Marines of the U.S. will not give up without a fight. Declared Marine Lt. Gen. P. X. Kelley, commander of America's front-line forces targeted for a Middle East conflict, "I'm not going to say whether we'll win, lose, or draw, but it will be a hell of a fight, I'll assure you."[4] Air Force Gen. Robert Mathis said recently, "Each side will beat each other to a pulp."[5]

The Distance Factor. The Soviets are only a country away from the Middle East. The U.S. is separated by oceans and thousands of miles. Two-thirds of the outnumbered U.S. contingent would have to be airlifted from Kentucky and North Carolina in the U.S.—some seven thousand miles away. It would take two weeks and as much as a month to mobilize, load, and inject the bulk of these troops into the battle zone. Meanwhile, the Marine Corps troops would have to be brought in from Diego Garcia, an island base twenty-two hundred miles distant. Less than 2,000 are at sea at any given time. Once there, they would have available only light weapons.

The Soviet Union has about 105,000 troops across the border in Afghanistan, four hundred miles from the vital Persian Gulf, and the remainder of its sizable armies lie just across the Iranian border in the Soviet homeland. The Soviet divisions could employ heavy tanks, artillery, armored vehicles, and other military hardware. Soviet air bases are also close by, giving the Soviets air superiority regardless of the better quality high-tech aircraft possessed by America.

The USSR has been preparing its forces in the region for war for a long time. Roads and highways to the borders have been built. British military observer Geoffrey Warhurst has stated, "The USSR did not spend twenty-five years and millions of dollars on roads and highways only so that one day it could take Afghanistan."

Soviet Enrichment. The Soviet Union has the capability of locking the beleaguered, outmanned U.S. forces in a vise grip. As former Army Chief of Staff General William C. Westmoreland has remarked, "The Russian moves on the chess board give every indication that the Soviet Union plans to encircle the oil-producing area of the Persian Gulf."

Just north of the Middle East lies the Soviet colossus itself; to the east is Afghanistan, a Soviet-controlled nation; southward are Soviet allies Ethiopia and Southern Yemen, and, due west, pro-Soviet Libya. It is very likely that in this war Iran would be an ally of Russia, so this will permit the Russian armies to begin their attack from an even closer vantage point.

Soviet Blitzkrieg Tactics. The element of surprise is very important to military victory, and the history of warfare shows that most nations that start wars win them. The world would undoubtedly be startled at the blitzkrieg strike by the Soviet forces. Surprise and blitzkrieg are tactics practiced to perfection by Soviet armed forces.

On January 2, 1980, Soviet commandos landed at the airport of Kabul, the Afghan capital. Airport authorities had been advised only that the Soviet transport aircraft arriving early that morning carried supplies and military equipment for the Afghan army—a part of the Soviet military aid program. The unsuspecting airport officials were shocked when the elite Soviet troops, armed to the teeth and riding in armored personnel carriers, burst forth from the huge aircraft and drove hurriedly away.

In only a few more minutes, the commandos had

seized the nearby government residence of Premier Hafizullah Amin, as well as the Kabul radio station and key military sites in the capital. Amin, his family, and his entire cabinet were summarily executed. Within days, every major Afghan city had fallen to the heavy Russian armor and tanks that followed the initial commando raid. Afghanistan was at the mercy of the Russian invaders.

So the Soviets forewarned the world of their ability to carry on a carefully planned and executed lightning-quick attack on a coveted target. We can be sure that the petroleum-laden lands of the Middle East will in a few years fall victim to the Soviets just as easily as did Afghanistan in 1980.

The Navy Equation. No longer can the United States count on mastery of the seas. This is especially true in the Mediterranean, the Indian Ocean, and the Persian Gulf areas near the Middle East. In 1981, Adm. Thomas Hayward, the top commander in the U.S. Navy, told a congressional committee that our navy is "overexposed and underinsured. Our margin of comfort is totally gone. We are operating at the ragged edge of adequacy."[6]

That same year former Chief of Naval Operations, Adm. Elmo R. Zumwalt, Jr., wrote an article for *International Security Review* entitled, "Naval Battles We Could Lose."[7] In it, he stated that the Soviets could successfully conduct a "short-grab" war in the Middle East in which the Russian naval forces provide the margin of victory. Stressing that "the U.S. Navy's position deteriorated dramatically during the last decade," Zumwalt said that it would take ten to fifteen years to

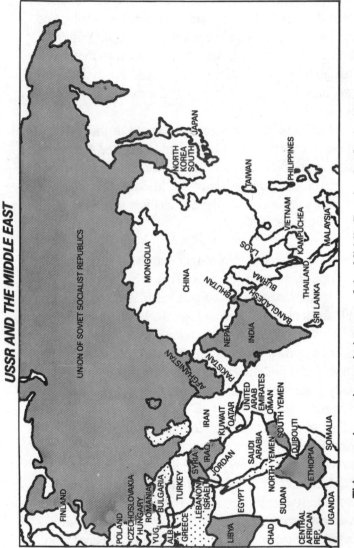

USSR AND THE MIDDLE EAST

This map shows the encirclement of the Middle East by the Soviet Union and its allies with whom it has formal treaties (shaded in gray). The Russians also have formidable naval fleets in all the waterways that surround this vulnerable region.

fully upgrade the U.S. Navy, and he encouraged the U.S. to move quicker than that to fix the problem.

In the past few years, our national leaders have heeded the warnings of men like Zumwalt and Hayward. Improvements have been made. But the Soviets also continue to improve their naval forces in the sea-lanes off the Middle East landmass. In the coming war, the once mighty U.S. Navy would face a formidable foe.

The Soviet Nuclear Edge. Russia now has nuclear superiority over the U.S. in most categories. According to the International Institute for Strategic Studies and the Department of Defense, here are comparisons for just a few key measures:

CATEGORY	U.S.	SOVIET UNION
Land-based missiles	1,049	1,398
Submarine-based missiles	576	989
Long-range bombers	312	140
Total launch platforms	1,937	2,527
Total explosive power (in megatons)	3,220	5,300

In Cuba, President John F. Kennedy forced Moscow to back down because of unchallenged U.S. nuclear superiority. Today, the Soviets lead in launchers (2,527 to the U.S.'s 1,937) and in explosive power (5,300 to our 3,220 megatons).

In the coming war, once the U.S. is forced to use nuclear weapons to prevent total defeat of its brave but outmatched contingent of ground forces, the resulting escalation will lead to major, all-out nuclear exchanges.

But, could the Soviets be the first to employ nuclear

weapons? Listen to the actual words of two Soviet military leaders, Gen.-Maj. N. Sushko and Col. S. A. Tyushkevicha. In 1965—over twenty years ago, *when the U.S. still had nuclear superiority*—these two Soviet strategists wrote these words in the Russian journal *Marxism-Leninism on War:*

> Bourgeois [United States] ideologists distort the question of the possible results of a thermonuclear war. They assert that in a modern war, there will be neither victories nor victors. Marxism-Leninism refutes these inventions and proves that in spite of the colossal sacrifices and losses which all the peoples of the world will suffer, the war will end with the destruction of imperialism.[8]

Over the years civilian Communist leaders in the USSR have repeatedly assured us that Russia loves peace and would never be the first to use nuclear bombs. But in Soviet military circles and within the policy-making councils of the Kremlin, the official philosophy expressed in 1965 by Sushko and Tyushkevicha still prevails. *Nuclear war is winnable*—so the party chiefs and military brass believe.

A series of studies by the U.S. Department of Defense and reported by Richard Foster, head of the Strategic Studies Center, in 1982, came to these important conclusions:

1. The Soviets are serious about *winning* a global nuclear war.

    2. The Soviet doctrine for victory calls for a *surprise*, pre-emptive, nuclear strike followed by a short but violent and decisive war.[9]

Thus, the Soviets may well choose to launch a pre-emptive nuclear missile and bomber attack on the U.S. homeland, the theory being that a surprise first strike may leave the U.S. so crippled that it cannot mount an effective counterattack. The Middle East ground and air invasion will be launched simultaneously.

FIFTEEN
THE NEW MILITARY POWERS: EUROPE, CHINA, AND JAPAN

We have left behind us the bipolar world in which two superpowers—the U.S. and the USSR—dominated and every country on earth fell in either of the two superpowers' camps. Instead, we have today a number of power centers—nations or combinations of nations—each of which has the potential to act independently to exert its will. These power centers include the giants of the East, Japan and China, and the nations of a revived Europe: West Germany, Britain, France, Italy, and others.

The New Europe and Asia. As World War II ended, a ravaged Europe was in tatters. A defeated, bomb-torn Germany was divided between East and West, and Italy was exhausted from its torturous existence under Mussolini. France's military had been battered by the Nazis and its economy weakened. The once great British Empire was in decline, and other European nations were undergoing reconstruction. Across the globe in Asia, China, ravaged by Japan, was in the early throes of all-out civil war between the forces of Chiang Kai-shek and the Communists under Mao's leadership. Meanwhile, a defeated Japan was being reorganized as American soldiers and sailors occupied the shores of that faraway land.

Now, four decades later, the nations of Europe bustle with economic activity. Gleaming new skyscrapers dot the skies of Rome, Frankfurt, and Munich. West Germany has become the world's fourth-largest industrial power, and German-built Mercedes, Porsche, and BMW autos race along the wide freeways that crisscross Europe. The leaders of the miraculously revived European states do not hesitate to criticize the United States, nor are they reluctant to defiantly assert their independence.

In Asia, we find Japan so economically powerful it rivals America in many areas of high technology. We also find that China can threaten Russia with a small but lethal nuclear-tipped missile force. This is a united China so influential that American presidents find it necessary to travel to Peking to keep diplomatic ties cordial and cohesive.

China is unafraid of either its neighboring colossus, the USSR, or its longtime capitalist adversary, the United States. Neither does Japan consider itself the inferior of the two superpowers. Indeed, Russia has charged Tokyo with reviving its pre-World War II militancy, while American leaders complain that the Japanese take unfair advantages in the world's trade markets.

A UNITED STATES OF EUROPE

Although there have been bitter past rivalries between the European nations, many Europeans, especially the political leaders, believe that the continent's destiny is to be united once again under the mantle of a single head of government. To achieve this goal, it is necessary to unshackle Eastern Europe from the chains imposed by the Soviet Union and cut the ties of Western Europe to the United States. These steps are, in fact, being taken. German and French leaders have established rapport with Moscow and seek bridges with East Germany, Poland, and other Communist Eastern European countries.

The European nations have taken several important steps toward political and economic unification. A joint European parliament has been formed. Though its powers are limited, there are plans to increase its authority over time. Financially and economically, the nations of Western Europe have both their European Economic Community (called Common Market) and a new common currency, used so far only by the banking and investment sectors of the economy.

In late 1985 eighteen European nations, led by France, Britain, and West Germany, formed a consortium called "Eureka." Eureka is a program in which the Europeans jointly undertake a number of research and development projects in such high-tech fields as robotics, lasers, and supercomputers. Its purpose: to keep the United States and Japan from outpacing Western Europe in high technology.

A UNITED EUROPEAN MILITARY

European leaders are taking the first steps to independence in the crucial area of defense. For over forty years Europe has joined with the U.S. and Canada in the collective military organization called the North Atlantic Treaty Organization (NATO). Now, signs indicate NATO may eventually break up. Franz Josef Strauss, one of Germany's most prominent politicians and head of its Christian Social Union Party, has said that "it is time that Germany be given a second key to the nuclear weapons stationed on our soil." This would, added Strauss, "make Germany independent of the United States." British Foreign Secretary Sir Geoffrey Howe, complaining about the U.S. invasion of Grenada in 1983, commented, "Europe needs an independent voice." And in a November 13, 1983, editorial in the conservative *Sunday Telegram* of London, commentator Peregruine Wostehorne argued for a "divorce" of European defense interests from those of America, claiming that Europeans should not place themselves at risk in a future nuclear war. Wostehorne was echoing the sentiment of France's Foreign Minister Claude Cheysson, who reportedly stated in 1982 that he was witnessing a "gradual divorce between Europe and America."

Meanwhile, the Associated Press in June 1983 reported that Western European defense ministers had denounced American domination of NATO's arms trade and warned that their countries would start buying less from U.S. manufacturers. This warning came about primarily because there is a resurgence of the European armaments industry. German and French arms and aerospace corporations are among the world's largest.

Few of the European leaders really have much confidence that, in the event of nuclear war, Washington, D.C., will sacrifice New York City or Dallas for, say, Paris or Brussels. Therefore, Europe has already begun to "go it alone" in many areas of defense. France pulled out of the NATO defense establishment years ago and today boasts of its own powerful nuclear strike force. France has five missile-carrying submarines, its own neutron bomb, and has developed a system of ground-based missiles capable of striking Soviet targets. Furthermore, Paris has pointedly stated that only Frenchmen will decide *when* and *where* this nuclear force is to be applied.[1]

FROM THE EAST

Incredible events are stirring in Asia, and the rest of the world had best keep its eyes on this vital region. The People's Republic of China—also called Red China or Communist China—has for over a decade made revolutionary changes in its economy and politics, tilting markedly toward capitalism and seeking ties with the United States. Meanwhile, China's neighbor, Japan, has become a mighty economic power whose high-tech prowess has caused envy—and alarm—in corporate boardrooms around the globe.

China and Japan are the two greatest nations in Asia today. China, with its huge 1 billion population, is the *only nation on earth* that could actually field an army of 200 million (see Rev. 9:15-16; 16:12). And Japan is the one country with the potential to build a technological fighting force anywhere near equal to that of the superpowers.

Both China and Japan have records of belligerency. In the past few decades, the Communists of Peking have had clashes with neighbors Vietnam, India, and Russia. They have swallowed up adjacent nations such as Tibet and Inner Mongolia, shelled Taiwanese islands, and fought a long, hard war with the Americans and United Nations forces in Korea.

Japan has been on a peaceful course since 1945, but it is not hard to imagine a future scenario in which, once again, the Empire of the Rising Sun will see fit to strike out in search of power and territory.

MUTUAL DISTRUST AND FEAR OF RUSSIA

Some ten years ago Gen. Edwin Starry, then commander of the U.S. Army in Europe, predicted that someday the United States and China would fight side-by-side against Soviet Russia. China and Russia have been bitter enemies for ages. Unfriendly as neighbors today, both claim lands in Siberia now occupied by the Soviets. In 1969, this territorial dispute turned into bloody warfare along the Usseri River, and hundreds of Chinese and Soviet troops were slain. The continuing dispute between China and Russia is one reason why Peking tilts toward the United States.

Japan also has its differences with Russia. While the U.S. ceded back to Japan Okinawa and other islands seized in World War II, Russia refuses to return the Japanese islands of Sakhalin and the Kuriles, which it also seized in the closing days of the war. Today, the Soviets have military bases on those islands, a festering sore for Tokyo. Those bases include a huge naval complex with missile-carrying submarines. From there, the new Soviet *Typhoon* operates; this tremendous 25,000-ton submarine carries nuclear warheads, and U.S. Intelligence says that twelve of those subs will soon operate in the seas off Japan and China.

China and Japan know also that over two thousand

Soviet combat aircraft and ten army divisions have been stationed in the regions in Russia nearest their countries' borders and that Soviet nuclear missiles are targeted in their direction. On occasion, the Soviets verbally threaten their Asian neighbors with destruction. Upset that Japan is now building up its defenses, *Tass,* the official Moscow news agency, released this hawkish threat to Japan in 1983:

> The authors of Tokyo's military plans make Japan a likely target for retaliation. . . . For such a densely populated island as Japan, this could spell a national disaster more serious than the one that befell it thirty-seven years ago [at Hiroshima and Nagasaki].

THE ORIENTAL ARMED FORCES

To counter the Soviet threat China has a large, standing military force which can be readily augmented by a trained people's militia. The Chinese also have a growing inventory of nuclear weapons and a limited number of missiles—the newest with multiple nuclear warheads—capable of hitting Soviet targets. Meanwhile, as one of the world's greatest technological powers, Japan has the capability of building an armed force second to none in its employment of high-tech weaponry.

Ominously, the Japanese *have* begun to devote more monies and attention to their defense. The defense budget has increased from a miniscule $2 billion in 1971 to over $12 billion in 1985. More is planned in the future. Premier Yasuhiro Nakasone has urged the Japanese Diet (Parliament) to spend an increasing amount for military needs. His nation's goal, declared the Japanese leader, is to make the islands of Japan into an "unsinkable aircraft carrier." Recent opinion polls show that the Japanese people strongly favor the rearmament plans of the government—in 1981 the figure was 82 percent of the people in favor of increased military spending.

Consequently, the Japanese are bringing more people into the armed services and are building modern fighter-bomber aircraft and advanced combat ships. Most experts believe that if a crash program were initiated, within five to seven years the Japanese could have one of the most formidable fighting forces in the world, second only to that of Russia and America.

JAPAN AND CHINA AS ALLIES

The Japanese and Chinese were enemies in World War II. But today Japan looks to China as a great trading partner. China reciprocates and hosts a growing number of Japanese businessmen and political leaders in Peking. In 1983 China became the top customer of Japan's large steel industries, and recently it was announced that Japan would construct a nuclear power plant in mainland China. Also, the Chinese buy computers, electronic equipment, and other technical supplies from Tokyo. These mutually beneficial ties will grow stronger in the coming years and will likely be the foundation upon which a military alliance will be founded.

THE SPIRIT OF WAR

Since the takeover of China by the Communists in 1949, China has consistently taken a militant stance in world affairs. Fearing both the Soviets and the Americans, Chairman Mao preached that "political power comes from the barrel of a gun." The Communists transformed China into a powerful military machine and made it a world nuclear power. In recent years the Chinese have mellowed in their attitude toward the United States, their goal being to acquire economic gain and military technology from the U.S. But China's leaders have let it be known to all that their country is willing and able to protect its interests in the world, by military force if necessary.

Japan adopted a pacifist policy after World War II, but in the past few years observers have noted a move back to militancy on the part of the Japanese. One expert, writing in 1983 for the magazine *Asia Week*, likened the current attitude to "Shogun Fever," pointing out that the ruthless spirit of the ancient Samurai warrior is being revived in modern Japan.[2]

Korea and the Philippines registered complaints last year after Japanese authorities rewrote school textbooks to delete references to Japanese militarism and atrocities in World War II. Protesters also were incensed when a Japanese movie, *The Empire of Greater Japan*, became a big hit. The movie glorifies wartime Prime Minister Tojo and blames the United States for the Japanese attack on Pearl Harbor.

Throughout the world, a growing column of experts shake their heads over the renewed militaristic spirit of the Japanese. In his best-selling book *The Japanese Mind: The Goliath Explained*,[3] Robert Christopher, an authority on Japan, states that behind their excruciatingly patient, polite exteriors the Japanese are intense, highly emotional people capable of violent explosions.

In another equally important book, just released, Australian author Russell Braddon comes to much the same conclusion. The title of his book is self-explanatory: *Japan against the World, 1941-2041: The Hundred Year War for Supremacy.*

For his book, Braddon interviewed leaders of such Japanese industries as Honda, Matsushita Electric, and Sony. His alarming discovery was that behind the Japanese economic miracle lies the same spirit that brought Japan its stunning victories in the early years of World War II. (Braddon notes that in Hirohito's 1945 message to the nation, the emperor did not use the term *surrender*. The Japanese, said the emperor, had merely decided to "stop fighting.")[4]

In *Japanese Militarism: Past and Present,*[5] a book published in America and based partly on unpublished sources from Japan, author Harold Hakwon Sunoo confirms the findings of Braddon, Christopher, and others. He explains the hazards of allowing a new wave of Japanese militarism and pleads with the West to monitor Japan's military activities.

Another scary sign of a Japanese revival of military spirit is the belief now taking hold among many Japanese that they are a superior race. Such a notion reminds us of the worst traits of human nature devoid of God's instincts for humanity and kindness. The *Wall Street Journal* reported one instance of the growing racial sentiment on November 19, 1982. Toshio Soejima, head of Japan's largest telecommunications firm, Nippon T & T Public Corporation, was quoted as saying:

> The Japanese are a people that can manufacture a product of uniformity and superior quality be-

cause the Japanese are a race of completely pure blood, not a mongrelized race as in the United States.

This comment from one of Japan's leading industrialists shocked many Western observers. To Japan's credit, it also dismayed some Japanese as well. In 1983, Kenchi Takemura, one of that country's most famous television commentators, criticized this attitude so prevalent among his countrymen. "The Japanese do not consider others human beings," he stated. "We tend to be insensitive to things not Japanese."

It is sad to read and hear that warlike, bigoted attitudes may be spreading in Japan. It is also sad, but true, that these attitudes are not confined to Japan. These attitudes can develop in any nation where God is not honored and where human pride takes precedence over divine law.

CONCLUSION

A book such as this is difficult to end. We have frankly discussed the ominous prospect of a World War III and the dangerous trend toward an immoral world that venerates science and technology but respects neither the holiness of God nor the rights of men. However, it would be inappropriate to conclude with a word of despair, for despair has no real place in the Christian life.

Perhaps it is best to pose some questions for the reader. First, *why* is man so determined to reshape his material world into a technological image? Second, will we be able to face the suffering that may come about as a result of man's misuse of technology and science? Finally, what can you and I, as Christians, do about the abuses of science and technology?

Fantastic new advances in science and technology certainly have the potential for enormous good. At the same time, these advances harbor the potential for dealing humanity unparalleled misery. Unfortunately, as Soviet exile Alexander Solzhenitzyn has so poignantly stated, modern man has forgotten God. Without the divine dimension, man cannot be expected to do otherwise than to practice selfishness, exhibit greed, and strive to exalt himself above his fellowman. This is why dictators come and go, people are often oppressed, and the nations of the world so quickly resort to conflict.

Science and technology provide the tools for man to realize his drive for self-power and control. As we master our environment and supply ourselves with sophisticated technological ornaments and devices, God seems to shrink in size and our own gait seems to stretch out over larger terrain. Science and technology make man self-contained. Perceiving himself to be master of his own, self-created universe, man need rely on no one but himself. No longer subject to physical limitations imposed on him by nature, man can finally succeed in becoming his own God.

Man sought conquest of the material world around him. Now he is achieving mastery of biological processes through genetic engineering. All that's left is the supernatural realm—the spiritual aspect of the universe. Conquest of the supernatural would be man's greatest achievement because it is the last obstacle to his seizing God status. But the Bible tells us that man's secular quest for dominance over the spiritual realm will end disastrously, for Satan has powers unimaginable to the human mind which, by comparison, is puny and hopeless. Ultimately, God is the final arbiter and master of both the spiritual and material realms. And the Bible makes it clear that neither prideful man nor Satan shall prevail.

Once man's scientific attitude is placed in perspective, we can better answer the question of whether we, as individuals, will be able to face the suffering that may well come about as a result of man's inevitable misuse of technology. The answer is a resounding yes, for the Scriptures promise that there is nothing that can separate us from the love of God and Christ (Rom. 8:31-39). We may suffer—indeed, Christians are already persecuted in many parts of the world, often with brutal abuse made possible by scientific advancements. But we cannot be torn apart from the loving God who, despite man's arrogance and technical prowess, still governs the world and ministers to our souls.

We may very well be approaching the end time. The fateful battle of Armageddon (discussed more fully in Appendix I) may not be far off. But we have the promise that God and those who love him will prove victorious, and the evil that leads to war, oppression, and other ills will be brought to nothing. And we have Christ's promise that we need never lose heart, for he has overcome the world and its sorrows (John 16:33).

Christ's promise and his love for us provide the keys to what we, as concerned Christians, must do about abuses of science and technology and the suffering and injustice that exist in a world that refuses to yield to the pleadings and invitation of a loving Creator. We must, first of all, put God first in our own lives and trust in his holy Word, the Bible. Then, infused with the power of the Holy Spirit, we must witness to sinners of Christ's reassuring promises and his love for them. To the best of our ability, even at the risk of our own lives and physical well-being, we must do what we can to make sure that technology and science are used for good and not for evil. Last, and most important, we must fervently pray that God's will be done on earth, for this is the prayer that our Lord Jesus Christ taught his disciples.

APPENDIX I
DOES THE BIBLE PROPHESY A MILITARY ARMAGEDDON?

A few years ago at the University of Texas where I was teaching a course on defense policy and international affairs, one of my students, a dedicated young Christian man, asked my permission to present an "unusual speech" to the class. His topic was "What God Has to Say about the End Times."

While the giving of a speech was a course requirement and the course did cover such topics as the balance of U.S./Soviet military power and the status of the Middle East, I was reluctant to permit a speech on biblical prophecy. After all, my officially assigned task was to teach the students an academic subject—American defense policy in the contemporary era—not what the Bible had to say. Just as our secular society deems it proper to keep prayer out of our elementary schools, so our society has judged it best to keep the teachings of the Bible out of university classrooms. According to the academic powers that be, mine was a university course, not a Bible study.

Thus it was unusual for the twenty-five students in my class to see and hear a fellow student speak of Isaiah and Revelation, Amos and Matthew. The young man spoke with sincerity and conviction. What he said was provocative, and afterward I asked the class what they thought of the speech and of biblical prophecy.

One student said that it was all "pure speculation"; another said that it was "irrelevant to the course." And yet another student—one of the brightest in the class—complained that "no one can understand the Bible" and that "we should stick to the facts in class."

"The Book of Revelation is all guesswork, anyway," chimed in a fellow student, "and subject to varying interpretation. Also, it's unscientific."

"Unscientific . . . pure speculation . . . guesswork . . . subject to varying interpretation." The words reverberated in my head. Is that what God's prophecies are? And is it true that "no one can understand the Bible?" Should I have allowed the speech or, as one of the students had commented, was the Bible indeed "irrelevant" to a college course on defense policy and international affairs?

My students' comments are typical, I believe, of the prevailing belief in America today. The Bible, people say, is not scientific; it is too complex to be understood, and it involves sheer guesswork because of differing interpretations. But these assertions are *not correct*. The fact is that the Bible is *not* that difficult to understand, and our comprehension involves more than mere guesswork. God is not the author of confusion, as Satan would lead modern man to believe.

THE PROBLEM OF INTERPRETATION

Consider the proposition that biblical prophecy is subject to differing interpretation. Actually, the problem of interpretation is minimized in the Bible by the *reinforcement* of Scripture. Different books in the Bible provide different data and images, and, taken together, the data and images reinforce each other and create a reasonably clear picture of God's will for man. Regardless of what mistaken laymen and even a few misguided ministers may say, the Bible does not contradict itself. Instead, study of the Bible in its entirety shows how it is possible to build a stable and precise picture by the process of reinforcement.

For instance, in studying the life and teachings of Jesus Christ, we are aided by the various accounts—by Matthew, Mark, Luke, and John. Each of the four Gospels provides a variety of rich details and a convincing documentation and proof of the other three.

Likewise, the Old Testament and New Testament again and again recount biblical prophecies which reinforce one another. Amos, Joel, Ezekiel, Matthew, Paul, Peter, John, and others demonstrate the consistency of Scripture in regard to prophecy. If we read Amos or Joel and fail to understand, we fortunately may compare the prophecies in those passages with those given elsewhere in the Bible. By doing this, the biblical student cannot fail to be astounded and gratified at the reinforcing nature of prophecy. By comparing the words of the prophets and the early Christian saints, we begin to understand the splendor and wisdom of God's Word and its inerrant nature.

Still, there are prophetic messages in the Bible that are indeed difficult to comprehend. Learned theologians argue mightily over their interpretation. But often the problem of understanding lies in the foibles of man. Bible scholars often try to read into biblical passages things that simply aren't there, or else they courageously attempt to force definitions and meaning from a passage that already is majestically clear.

Let me illustrate. In Luke 17:20, 21, Jesus answers those who ask him about the kingdom of God. Expecting to hear descriptions of when the kingdom would appear and what it would look like, the questioners were amazed to hear Jesus say, "The kingdom of God is within you."

This response was probably so unexpected that it astounded the Jews of his day. Yet Jesus' answer was profound. Like Jesus' listeners then, modern man often evaluates God's Word from his own limited perspective. And biblical understanding suffers as a result.

THE PROBLEM OF SYMBOLISM

One of the areas where Bible readers confront the most difficulty is in the interpretation of symbolism. While the use of symbolism in prophecy admittedly hinders our understanding, this should not be a stumbling block for the Christian who truly desires to comprehend God's message to our generation.

Again, turn to the pages of the Bible itself to receive a proper understanding of what a particular symbolic passage means and what the symbols represent. Note that symbols in the Bible are almost always followed by a *biblical* interpretation. For instance, the Old Testament prophet Daniel had a vision (Dan. 7) of four great beasts arising from the sea, one as a lion, the second like a leopard, the third resembling a bear, and the fourth radically different in that it had great iron teeth and ten horns. This fourth beast was ferocious and terrible, and devoured those in its path.

Daniel himself, one of the wisest men in the world at that time, was perplexed over this vision. However, in the same chapter we see that angels later interpreted to Daniel the dream of the four beasts (Dan. 7:15-27). The four beasts, an angel explained, were four great kings which would arise. And the fourth beast—the most dreadful— was a king (the Antichrist) who in the latter days would devour the whole earth and make war with the saints. Daniel was shown how the king would eventually be destroyed by God.

If we turn to other prophetic passages in the Bible (Rev. 13; 17:12-18; 19; Matt. 24:15; 2 Thess. 2:8-9; and others) the full meaning of the symbols in Daniel's vision comes into focus. All provide reinforcement.

SYMBOLIC VERSUS LITERAL INTERPRETATION

It should be noted, however, that many of the events and things described in biblical prophecies which appear to be symbolic are in actuality descriptions of *literal* phenomena. There are many examples in the Bible where the prophets furnished a literal description of a vision or event which, to early Christians, must have appeared either symbolic or mysterious.

For example, the prophets describe in Revelation, Ezekiel, Isaiah, and other books the workings of technological weapons of war which, before our current generation, were the province of dreamers and science fiction writers. The prophets naturally did not use twentieth-century terminology. Instead they described how these weapons looked to them and what their effects were.

The phenomenal descriptions of the Bible's prophets are disparaged and given short shrift today, chiefly because of the prophets' failure to use the modern terms employed by modern military scientists. It is a mistake to think that men who lived two thousand to three thousand years ago would cast their descriptions of weapon systems in modern terms. They used the only words they had to describe phenomena unfamiliar to them.

It is wise to keep in mind that the first telephones were called "mechanical talking devices," that early automobiles were characterized as "horseless carriages" and that the airplane of the Wright brothers was called a "flying machine" in early press reports. In fact, the Smithsonian Institution placed a sign on an early aircraft which read: "First Heavier-than-Air Machine Capable of Flight."

In 1965, while visiting a remote village in northeast Thailand, old men there told me through an interpreter of the first plane they ever saw. "It was during the war with Japan," said one of the villagers. "I was in the rice fields and I heard a loud noise. When I looked overhead, I saw a large, iron bird with big wings. It shone in the sun and scared me."

That comment was by an old man, unschooled in modern terminology, living in an isolated village that did not at that time have roads, motor vehicles, or even electricity. He referred to the plane as a *bird* because it was the only apt word in his vocabulary. In many ways his situation was like that of the prophets, for they likewise did not have a grounding in our technical terminology: missile, laser, airplane, tank, and so forth.

As progress continues to be made in twentieth-century tools of warfare, the incredible accuracy of the prophetic visions comes more clearly into focus. Our generation is privileged, for while earlier Christians accepted these prophecies on faith, we now see the evidence. Prophecy is being realized before our very eyes.

Thus in Revelation 9:17-19 John's vision of a massive army of men advancing on "horses" which breathed fire, smoke, and brimstone was inexplicable until this century when the battle tank and the helicopter gunship were rushed into combat. Seemingly, these modern weapons with their powerful cannon and rockets fit John's description.

If we had John's prophecy only, we would not discount the possibility that the warfare he envisioned was fought with technologically advanced machines. But the Bible provides significant reinforcement in prophecies by Joel, Nahum, Isaiah, and other Old and New Testament prophets.

Nahum vividly described scenes of a latter-day conflict that would take place just prior to Jesus' triumphant return:

> He that dasheth in pieces is come up . . . the chariots
> shall be with flaming torches in the day of his prepara-
> tion, and the fir trees shall be terribly shaken. The
> chariots shall rage in the streets, they shall jostle
> against one another in the broad ways: they shall seem
> like torches, they shall run like the lightnings. (Nah.
> 2:1, 3, 4)

It seems likely that Nahum's prophetic vision was of modern-day battle tanks—powerful battle weapons resembling chariots with guns that "seem like torches" and the brute strength to bulldoze right through stands of fir trees. With speeds approaching those of automobiles, the M-1 can "run like the lightnings" with its rockets and guns ablaze.

For even more reinforcement, we should read from the Book of Joel:

> The appearance of them is as the appearance of horses; and as horsemen, so shall they run. Like the noise of chariots on the tops of mountains shall they leap, like the noise of a flame of fire that devoureth the stubble. . . . They shall climb the wall like men of war; . . . and they shall not break their ranks. . . . and when they fall upon the sword, they shall not be wounded. . . . (Joel 2:4-8)

The prophets may not have been familiar with the terms *tank* and *helicopter,* but they certainly provided a working description of such machines. Furthermore, we see that, according to Joel 2:4, the objects have "the appearance of horses." Note the word *appearance!* Here again we see the value of studying and evaluating *all* the prophecies of the Bible rather than selectively interpreting a single passage.

Some critics of biblical prophecy demand that if John and Joel used the term *horse,* we must assume they meant a living, breathing creature of four legs, bountiful hair, and flowing mane. The critics laugh, pointing out that in an age of high-technology machines, tanks, and motor vehicles it is highly unlikely that combat troops would ride real horses into battle.

Such critics and unbelievers bring to mind the Jews of Jesus' time who were incapable of comprehending how the kingdom of God could be *inside* a person. Such narrow literalism makes the Bible smaller than it should be and an impediment to intelligent, thoughtful understanding.

Now it is true, of course, that God *could* bring forth the miracle of huge numbers of horses to be used by armies. After all, he is God and all things are possible with him. However, he certainly will not perform such a miracle simply because of an unyielding and inflexible interpretation of the Bible by men here on earth. God is in charge of events; man isn't.

Perhaps the solution here would be to seek to expand the boundaries of our own vision while praying and asking God to lend understanding to what we read. The difficulty of interpretation lies not in God's Word, but in our own human frailty.

I do not wish to be dogmatic, but I am convinced that if we truly seek an understanding of God's Word, we must admit the possibility that biblical authors prophesied about modern military weapons. In fact, biblical prophecy seems remarkably accurate in its descriptions of modern technological weapon systems. The figure below provides biblical references that often astonish with their clarity and detail.

PROPHECY AND THE WEAPONS OF ARMAGEDDON

WORLD WAR III WEAPONS	BIBLICAL REFERENCES
Chemical-Biological Agents	**Isaiah** 1:6; 9:20; 15:6; 17:11; 18:5 **Jeremiah** 8:3; 8:14 **Ezekiel** 7:15; 12:18-19 **Joel** 1:10-20 **Nahum** 2:10 **Habakkuk** 3:17 **Zephaniah** 1:17 **Revelation** 8:10-11; 9:3-11; 11:5-6; 16:2-4; 16:10-11

Weather-Altering Devices	**Jeremiah** 25:32 **Ezekiel** 13:13-14 **Zechariah** 14:17-18 **Matthew** 24:7 **Luke** 21:25 **Revelation** 8:5; 11:6
Neutron Bombs	**Zephaniah** 1:12-13
Nuclear Warheads	**Isaiah** 1:7; 2:19; 5:25; 5:30; 9:5; 9:19; 13:5; 13:10; 13:13; 14:17; 24:6; 24:16-23; 29:5-6; 30:13-17; 30:30 **Jeremiah** 4:24-27; 9:10-11; 26:18; 49:21; 50:32 **Ezekiel** 6:6; 12:20; 38:20-22 **Joel** 2:2; 2:10; 2:31; 3:16 **Amos** 8:9; 9:5 **Micah** 1:4 **Nahum** 2:6 **Zephaniah** 1:2-3; 1:15-18 **Zechariah** 14:7; 14:12-15 **Matthew** 24:21-22; 24:29 **Revelation** 6:12-14; 8:7-9; 16:8-12; 16:18-21
Tanks and Armor	**Isaiah** 10:34 **Jeremiah** 4:13 **Ezekiel** 14:15; 38:4 **Daniel** 7:7 **Joel** 2:2-10 **Amos** 1:3 **Nahum** 2:1-4 **Revelation** 9:3-19
Aircraft and Missiles	**Isaiah** 14:29-30 **Jeremiah** 4:13; 49:22 **Ezekiel** 1:1-24 **Zechariah** 5
Space Weapons (Laser Rays/ Energy Beams)	**Isaiah** 34:5-7 **Ezekiel** 39:6 **Joel** 2:3; 2:30 **Nahum** 3:15 **Luke** 17:29-30 **Revelation** 8:12; 13:13

In the ancient world of the Hebrew prophets, centuries before the birth of Jesus Christ, warfare was simple and unfettered by sophisticated armaments. Men, horses, chariots, swords, bows and arrows, lances and, on occasion, battering rams and catapults—these were the mainstay of armies. Gunpowder was not invented until about A.D. 700, in China, so rifles, cannons, and other such weapons were nonexistent in the days of Daniel, Ezekiel, and the other prophets of God.

Isn't it incredible, then, that over twenty-five hundred years ago, these inspired men would prophesy about a future war in which weapons would be employed that so closely resemble the workings of today's high-tech instruments of warfare?

BIBLE PROPHECIES FORETELL A NUCLEAR ARMAGEDDON

Does the Bible warn us of the effects of nuclear weapons to be unleashed in the last days? A compelling case can be made that the Bible prophesies a nuclear Armageddon. For example, Zephaniah described the great day of the Lord as "a day of wasteness and desolation, a day of darkness and gloominess, a day of clouds and thick darkness" (Zeph. 1:15). Isaiah prophesied that in the latter days cities would be totally destroyed "even to the dust" following a blast of "heat with the shadow of a cloud" (Isa. 25:5, 12).

The prophecies of Zephaniah and Isaiah paint a picture of the reality of a future nuclear holocaust. Isaiah also tells future generations of the *suddenness* of nuclear strikes. The blast, he says, will be upon its victims quickly and without warning: "it shall be at an instant suddenly" (Isa. 29:5).

In his book *Hiroshima*, noted author John Hersey described the torrid aftereffects of the atomic blast on hapless human victims:

> Their faces were wholly burned, their eye sockets were hollow, the fluid from their melted eyes had run down their cheeks.

In Zechariah 14:12 we find a chilling prophecy that matches almost word for word Hersey's description of nuclear effects on the bodies of victims:

> And this shall be the plague wherewith the LORD will smite all the people that have fought against Jerusalem; their flesh shall consume away while they stand upon their feet, and their eyes shall consume away in their holes, and their tongue shall consume away in their mouth.

There are many, many other Bible prophecies which seem to apply to the heat and raging infernos generated by nuclear blasts and the great destruction to come following a world nuclear conflict:

> Your country is desolate, your cities are burned with fire. (Isa. 1:7)
>
> For then shall be great tribulation, such as was not since the beginning of the world to this time, no, nor shall ever be. (Matt. 24:21)
>
> And I will show wonders in the heavens and in the earth, blood, and fire, and pillars of smoke. (Joel 2:30)
>
> But the same day that Lot went out of Sodom it rained fire and brimstone from heaven, and destroyed them all. Even thus shall it be in the day when the Son of man is revealed. (Luke 17:29-30)
>
> Therefore the inhabitants of the earth are burned, and few men left. (Isaiah 24:6)
>
> And I will kindle a fire in his cities, and it shall devour all round about him. (Jer. 50:32)
>
> The mountains shall be thrown down, and the steep places shall fall, and every wall shall fall to the ground. (Ezek. 38:20)

These prophetic images rival any description of the effects of nuclear weapons found in military textbooks. These references are not about a war of swords and lances or of hand-to-hand combat. It seems clear that the prophets of old were describing nuclear war—as revealed to them by God. If nothing else would cause a person to believe in God and the truth of his prophecies, *this* should.

ARE THE BIBLE'S PROPHECIES SCIENTIFIC?

An accusation often voiced by unbelievers is that the Bible is illogical; that it has no relevance in an age of computers and high technology. *Unscientific* is the word some use. The weary arguments about evolution refuting the Bible are brought to mind. Upon close examination, these assaults on the Bible—and also its prophecies—are neither scientific nor intellectually sound. The principles of science—of empirical fact and reason—are friends to the Bible, not foes.

Christians sometimes are forced on the defensive by agnostics and unbelievers who challenge them to "prove" the Bible. Sorrowfully, Christians often resort to saying that the Bible must be taken on faith and not evidence.

But this is not completely true. Whereas faith is supremely important (see chapter 7 of Hebrews), faith and fact are not mutually exclusive.

For example, we accept Jesus as the Son of God by faith, but his works on earth and the witness of those who were with him demonstrate the proof of both his existence and his divinity. If we are to deny that Jesus will one day return to rule earth, we must also be forced to deny these same sources of factual evidence, as well as the unerring words of the prophets. That Jesus lived—and lives—is *fact*. It is also an article of Christian *faith* that we believe in these facts. Furthermore, if we accept the inerrancy of God's Word—and as Christians we must—we cannot but conclude that Jesus will return, for numerous biblical passages assure us of his Second Coming.

THE LOGIC AND WISDOM OF THE BIBLE

The Bible is truly an incredible volume containing sixty-six books by dozens of contributing authors—all led by God. It is also the most accurate and revealing history book ever compiled. And the most amazing fact of all is its prophecy. It is easy to understand why Nebuchadnezzar marveled over Daniel's prophetic revealing of dreams and why the kings of old were moved to wrath by the proclamations of Jeremiah and other divinely inspired prophets. The reason is clear: the prophecies were meaningful and logical, and the prophets' insights into military and political affairs were unparalleled.

The biblical prophets cut to the very heart of an issue. Their level of education was immaterial, for they possessed the wisdom of the Most Holy. Led by God, their in-depth knowledge of man's behavior and his affairs was astounding. In effect, the biblical prophets were the consummate political scientists of their day, unrivaled and uncanny experts on the subjects they prophesied on, for it was God's will that they spoke with authority.

It is well to keep in mind the supernatural genius and masterful knowledge displayed by Jesus Christ while he was on earth. In the use of fact and evidence our Lord was unbeatable, and his indisputable logic finally caused the scoffers and doubters to hold their tongues.

PROPHECY'S VALUE TODAY

The logic of the Bible extends even to the most profound issues of our own day. The social conditions under which we live and the internal and external enemies we face are *factually* covered in the Bible. And this is why prophecy is so important. God's promises to man, in particular the promises of the Second Coming of Christ and the promises of eternal life, are fully outlined throughout his Word. While we accept Jesus into our hearts through faith, we know without a shadow of a doubt the certainty of his return and the guarantee of his promises.

CHRIST'S VICTORY IS OUR VICTORY

Some believe Armageddon to be the final battle—that is, it will mean the end of the world. This is inaccurate. God will not allow the world to be totally destroyed. Even though Armageddon and the worldwide conflict that surrounds its occurrence will be ghastly and will exact a grim toll of casualties, all of mankind will not be extinguished. Instead, by the grace of God, these days of woe will be summarily ended:

> And except those days should be shortened, there should no flesh be saved: but for the elect's sake those days shall be shortened. (Matt. 24:22)

As the armies of Armageddon converge and engage one another, Christ will intervene. Revelation 19:11-21 describes how Christ will destroy the assembled armies, then take and cast the Beast and his False Prophet into a lake of fire burning with brimstone.

These verses in Revelation that prophesy the Second Coming of Christ are central to the Christian faith. A number of revisionist theologians, liberal teachers, and New Age leaders have proposed that Jesus cannot possibly return to earth. To them, our Lord was a mere mortal with a worthy message for his times. Many theologians and pastors also deny the Virgin Birth and the Trinity.

Don't be misled. The Bible could not be more clear! Jesus is coming. He will defeat Satan and his angels and reign supreme.

THE KINGDOM OF JESUS

Having conquered the Beast and his hordes, Jesus will establish his kingdom on earth (Rev. 20:4-6). This has to be the most blessed and joyful event of all time: the ascension of Christ to the throne of the planet Earth. Satan offered him this kingdom long ago; "Worship me," said the Evil One, "and all this is yours." Jesus refused. But now, after Armageddon, the Son of God claims his kingdom on his own terms.

Jesus will not only come as a conqueror and a king, but as a liberator and a judge. He will open the Book of Life and judge the living and the dead. This is the vision (Rev. 21) which John was given of the new world to come after God's Day of Judgment and of the reward to be given the believers in God:

> And I heard a great voice out of heaven saying, Behold, the tabernacle of God is with men, and he will dwell with them, and they shall be His people. . . . And God shall wipe away all tears from their eyes; and there shall be no more death, neither sorrow, nor crying, neither shall there be any more pain, for the former things are passed away. And he that sat upon the throne said, Behold, I make all things new.

THE PLAN OF SALVATION

Jesus Christ promised that all those who believe in him, repent of their sins, and call on his name will be saved. To these men and women are reserved heavenly rewards and life eternal. Throughout this book, I have sought to show that the fulfillment of prophecy is proof of God's love for you and for me. God's desire is not that we suffer or that we perish. Instead, he calls us to salvation and to joy and happiness through his Son, Jesus Christ: "Worship God: for the testimony of Jesus is the spirit of prophecy" (Rev. 19:10).

If you are not at present a Christian and a believer in God and his promises, I fervently pray you will read and carefully consider the following verse, John 3:16. In this one wonderful sentence is God's plan of salvation for you.

> For God so loved the world, that he gave his only begotten Son, that whosoever believeth in him should not perish, but have everlasting life.

APPENDIX II
THE NEW AGE MOVEMENT: A SCIENTIFIC RELIGION FOR THE END TIME?

History demonstrates that an age of barbarism cannot be ushered in until a society is fully ready. A religious or philosophical system must first take hold and motivate a small, elite group to generate social upheaval and change in an all-out struggle for dominance and power. This was the pattern in 1917 when Lenin and his Bolsheviks seized power in Russia and later in the 1930s when Hitler and his Brown Shirts subverted and seduced the German citizenry through flattery, propaganda, and intimidation. Both the Communists and the Nazis claimed that objective science supported their corrupt new cultural system.

Today, the United States and the world face yet another great social movement—a system that combines the worst of science, economics, and psychology in a dangerous new formulation. This powerful modern day successor to communism and Nazism, often called "the New Age Movement" by some writers, uses an insidious, compelling tool that previous barbaric systems failed to wield: the color of religious revelation.

In this appendix we'll examine this new religion and discover its darker side. As you will see, this religion immerses itself in a false science and offers to a reprobate world the promise that salvation lies in technology.

A RELIGIOUS SCIENCE FOR THINKING PEOPLE

In the New Age worldview, science and technology provide magnificent tools which man can use to enhance his own powers of mind. In reality, science and technology are abused by New Age teachers who falsely claim that their error-filled and improbable doctrines are based on scientific fact. They claim that a belief in the Bible and in Jesus Christ is unscientific and unbecoming for intellectuals and thinking people. For example, in her book *Towards a New World Religion,* Lola Davis says that a New Age world religion "is needed to meet the spiritual needs of thinking people, to synthesize scientific knowledge with spiritual teachings, and to unify mankind." Then Davis takes her case one step further by proclaiming that "revelations of God . . . include both spiritual and scientific knowledge."[1]

This can be heady stuff for scientists. They are led to believe that their scientific theories are, in fact, *divine revelations.* But we know from studying the history of scientific development that scientific theories are never established as absolute truth, for they constantly undergo revision. What is "truth" today becomes outmoded and inaccurate tomorrow. At one time or another, scientists have delivered to the world ironclad "truths" to the effect that airplanes will never fly, that computers could never be built to rival the human mind in calculating speed, that polio could never be conquered. Louis Pasteur, Madame Curie, and the Wright brothers were once branded as scientific fakers or worse by scientists who pointed to accepted scientific "truths" that supposedly refuted the early findings of those brilliant scientists and inventors. Even the century-old theory of evolution is today undergoing dramatic revision, for the archaeological, biological, and geological facts demonstrate that Charles Darwin, who first propounded the theory of evolution, could not have been wholly correct in his assumptions.

The wise scientist knows scientific truths are ever-changing and that science itself is nothing more than a continuous, never-ending search for the truth—not the truth itself, but the search for truth. God, however, does not market theories nor experiment at learning scientific "truths." God is immutable. He knows all, and to him there is no mystery unrevealed. But today, thousands of scientists are being intellectually seduced into believing that their theories are "divine" revelations, truths derived from their own godlike intellect, produced through achieving an inner state of higher consciousness.

Scientists not versed in the Scriptures nor aware of the biblical warnings regarding human pride and the apostasy of a pseudo-science cannot help but be thrilled to hear a New Age herald like Lola Davis declare that the new world religion is one in which separate religions disappear as "religion will come to be recognized as a scientific process." Furthermore, Davis asserts, "science has already enlarged man's concept of God."

The New Age world religion promises to unify science and religion and demolish the wall that separates secular and divine, material and spiritual. It boldly seeks to marry secular science and the material realm to religion. This has also been Satan's primary goal.

TAKING SIDES: SCIENCE TURNS TO THE EAST

For centuries, scientists have held that to remain objective, science must be neutral toward religions. But scientists are now beginning to take sides. Noted physicist Fritjof Capra, in his best-selling book *The Tao of Physics*, enthusiastically endorses the New Age worldview while rejecting Christianity as antiscience and out of step with the modern world. "The classical ideal of scientific objectivity," says Capra, "can no longer be maintained."[2] In its place, Capra and a growing number of other scientists propose that science adopt the Eastern religions (Buddhism, Hinduism, and Taoism) and mysticism. Capra also maintains that the roots of physics and of all Western science are to be found in the first period of Greek philosophy in the sixth century B.C., when science, philosophy, and religion were not separated.

Capra fails to fully acknowledge that from that same era came beliefs in spiritism, animism, polytheism, homosexual behavior as an acceptable life-style, the concept of the universe as a divine, living entity (pantheism), and such atrocities as human bondage, slavery, and infanticide. Yet Capra states that Greek and Eastern beliefs and practices provide "a conception of the world in which scientific discoveries can be in perfect harmony with spiritual and religious beliefs."

The turn of science toward the East and its mystical religions is only one manifestation of a wholly new revolution in science which threatens to discredit and destroy Christianity. Many scientists work fervently to bring about this destruction; others, more naive, are simply ignorant of the implications of their research. Claiming to be objective, they present new scientific theories and concepts without malice, unaware that others twist the truth and incorporate these new findings into their unholy doctrine. Many scientists would be particularly shocked to discover their theories being used to assert the superiority of Eastern religion and mysticism—and even the occult—over the Judeo-Christian concepts of God and religion.

If the New Age challenge to Christianity was only a matter of arrogant scientific opposition to the Bible, the present danger might not be so real. But the New Age embrace of the occult and Eastern mysticism is alarming.

Many New Age congregations and group members are eager and willing to dabble in and seriously practice an incredible hodgepodge of strange and bizarre religious ceremonies and rituals. Almost anything *but* a personal God, Jesus Christ, and real Christianity is acceptable to the New Age believer.

PANTHEISM—WORSHIPING THE DIVINE UNIVERSE

The New Age religion is similar in many ways to the ancient belief system called *pantheism*. Pantheists deny the existence of a personal God, maintaining that the universe itself is god. What's more, they claim that the human mind is an integral part of the web that is the universe, and that the human mind *is* the universe.

If for New Agers no personal God exists, and if man is himself God, there can be no place called heaven where God and his Son, Jesus, and all his mighty angels reside. Nor can there be a hell with a devil and his spirits. Heaven and hell are regarded by New Agers as primitive, outmoded concepts.

Some New Age writers claim that the pantheistic concept of the universe as God is consistent with new scientific thought. The New Physics, they point out, suggests that the only reality that exists is in our heads. When we gaze at the universe, we merely gaze at a projection of our own minds. Furthermore, the New Physics (also called quantum mechanics) contends that our minds connect with, and are inseparable from, the whole universe, being holistic and similar to threads in a spider's web. Science writer Bob Toben and scientist Fred Alan Wolf, in *Space Time and Beyond*, seek to explain that "the whole of the universe, all knowledge, is contained within each individual and each thing." They conclude, "We are influenced by the stars. We are the stars."[3]

Intellectuals now teach the New Physics in our universities and colleges. I recall a conversation I once had with one of my brightest university students. A natural sciences major, he had been very impressed by a physics professor who had recently delivered a lecture on "astrology and quantum mechanics."

"I now believe," said the earnest young man, "that astrology is quite possibly scientific fact." He went on to describe what he felt he had learned—that the entire cosmos is interconnected and that everything in the universe somehow affects every other part. "It's clear that the movement of heavenly bodies sets off vibrations that influence man's behavior," he solemnly pronounced.

"So you are convinced that our destiny is in the stars?" I asked.

"Yes. Exactly."

"I'm sure you heard that from the physics professor," I said, "but it's not true. Your destiny and mine are in the hands of God. The stars are there for other purposes."

"But according to the New Physics," he exclaimed, somewhat frustrated, "the stars *are* God."

Looking intently into his eyes, I thought a moment, then responded: "God *made* the stars."

DID THE UNIVERSE CREATE ITSELF?

Many scientists would not agree with me. Quite a few insist that the universe created itself! Colin Wilson, an occult author, comments in a preface to *The Intelligent Universe: A Cybernetic Philosophy* (by David Foster) that "the universe itself may not be a dead thing; . . . perhaps it is alive and intelligent and this living universe coded [itself] and continues to code, program, and control everything in the universe."[4] Inside this remarkable but flawed book, author David Foster theorizes that the world is like a gigantic electronic computer. Man is envisioned as only a computer component that networks with, or links into, the universal computer.

But, according to Foster, man has the inherent capability to achieve autonomy from his creator and controller: the master computer that is the universe itself. Through the exercise of higher consciousness, Foster explains, man can rise up and become master of the universe (i.e., "God"). Again, we see in operation the belief that man is divine and can realize his divine nature merely by expanding his conscious mind.

Like many other New Age scientists, Foster is a believer in science as a panacea for modern man. He says that with the theories of Galileo, "Science replaced religion as a more sure touchstone to reality." Finally today, due to the revelations of the New Physics and continuing scientific and technological discoveries, science and religion must come together. However, only a *new religion* will do, says Foster. To try to mix the new science with outdated religions such as Christianity will only lead to a "botched-up affair," he cautions. Therefore, Foster invites "open-minded scientists and open-minded religious men to join me in a common boat . . . on to an ocean of quite new ideas."

According to Foster, these new ideas must include the doctrine that the purpose of the universe is to become more intelligent and, likewise, the purpose of man is to become more intelligent. A religion with intelligent man at the pinnacle as God and Lord of all he surveys is a key principle of Foster's proposed New World religion.

More and more scientists follow Foster's pattern in enthroning the universe itself—nature—as god. Physicist Heinz R. Pagels (*The Cosmic Code*), for example, supports religious conversions based on the new god of nature: "If there are those who claim a conversion experience through reading scripture, I would point out that the book of nature also has its converts . . . scientists have unleashed a new force in our social, political, and economic development—perhaps *the major force*."

Many scientists would have us believe that an intelligent universe created itself out of nothingness and that man's mind power can reshape the world into any fashion it desires. But Albert Einstein, perhaps this century's greatest scientist, professed otherwise. Einstein was a believer in a transcendent

God. He often stated that the universe could not have been created without an observer. And as to the concept of a malleable, changeable universe, Einstein stated simply, "God does not play dice with the universe."

Just as objective science refutes the universe as its own creator, there is not one shred of evidence that our minds (thought) are part of a universal force field and that we can somehow tap into that field with only the exercise of our raw intelligence. An analogy is the existence of electromagnetic fields. Electrical signals are everywhere, but we need instruments (radio, TV, magnets, telephone) to bring them in. Gravity is also a force, but no way has been found to tap into it. Likewise, even if a unified force field of energy does exist, as well it might, there is no proof that our human minds are adequate of themselves to bring in and send signals.

A NEW THEORY: EVOLUTION OF CONSCIOUSNESS

Another cornerstone of the New Age world religion is a firm belief in the theory of *evolution*. But wait! Most scientists do not intend to continue the protracted debate about whether or not man descended from apes or monkeys. Most readily admit that Darwin's theories are in sore need of revision. They subscribe to newer theories of evolution, in particular the theory of *punctuated equillibria* first articulated in the Soviet Union in the early 1970s.

According to this theory, species can develop very quickly. It does not take millions of years of random selection for a new species such as man to evolve. Instead, an entirely new species can arise over a period of only tens of thousands of years. Adding to this new theory, New Agers believe that an evolutionary leap can occur spontaneously and instantaneously. This theory of spontaneous, super-rapid evolution has become known as *transformational evolution*.

Surprisingly, this theory of transformational evolution seems to square with the biblical account of near-instantaneous creation as described in the Book of Genesis. However, New Age thought excludes the possible confirmation of Scripture. What concerns many secular teachers is the idea that modern man might be on the precipice of an incredible evolutionary leap. They suggest that man's current state of development is a prelude to the next higher level of evolution, a level in which man's mind vaults into a new, higher consciousness.

This startling theory holds that as more human beings become more conscious and aware of their own divine nature and their latent powers within, a *critical mass* of energy will develop. This critical mass will break through the evolutionary threshold and a new *cosmic consciousness* will envelop the globe. Transformed into Superman, *Homo sapiens* will become a new species: literally a race of gods.

In essence, man's scientific destiny is to evolve into a higher order of consciousness. Enlightened man shall be the ruler of the universe and his own god. He shall unite with the universe and he and it shall become one.

A CHALLENGE TO THE HOLY WORD

The theory of transformational evolution is a direct challenge to the Word of God. It denies the Genesis account of creation and maintains that creation is a continuing process of nature. It alleges that all truth is relative and subject to evolutionary change, and it denies absolutes.

Worse than these untruths, however, is the unholy claim that the end purpose of this continuing evolutionary and transformational process is the deification of man. Many people believe that a new, superhuman race of man-gods is just around the corner. This race of superintelligent beings will exalt the mind and be consistent with modern science and technology.

When will this new race, already emerging, complete its evolutionary metamorphosis and spring into existence? Some writers claim that it will only come after the earth has been "cleansed" of those negative forces—such as fundamentalist Christianity—which today remain as obstacles to the new world order of science, technology, and religion.

Charles Lumsden, an evolutionary biologist at the University of Toronto, believes that "the end of the twentieth century will be the Great Age of the Mind."[6] Ruth Montgomery, known by her millions of readers as the Herald of the New Age, has said in her book *Threshold to Tomorrow* that "planet earth is currently on the cusp between the Piscean and Aquarian Ages." Montgomery says that her inner spirit guides have confided to her that "we are indeed on the threshold of a New Age, which the guides say will be ushered in by a shift of the earth on its axis at the close of this century." Once this New Age is ushered in, "The souls who helped to bring on the chaos of the present century will have passed into spirit to rethink their attitudes, and the new race will engage in peaceful pursuits and the uplifting of spirits."

Evidently, according to Montgomery, fundamentalist Christians and other "heretics" and troublemakers will simply be banished to another dimension where, she says, they can be taught the truths of the New Age by the spirits that inhabit that dimension and who have not yet been reincarnated. Richard Spangler, a prominent New Age leader and head of the Lucis Trust, has echoed Montgomery. He, too, has threatened that less enlightened, inferior men may have to be sent to another dimension, where they can be "more happy."

These bizarre statements by Montgomery, Spangler, and other New Age leaders suggest that, if the New Age juggernaut continues to steamroll toward world domination, an ominous age of persecution for Christians lies just ahead.

Adolph Hitler made similar muddled statements in the 1930s—statements about how, once he had gained power, his Third Reich would solve the problems of a lesser and inferior species. The result was a network of concentration camps and the torturous deaths of 6 million Jews and tens of millions of other innocents. Christians would do well to be aware that the Church may find itself persecuted because Christians are perceived by the governing authorities as threats to the social order. This is already true in many Communist bloc countries, and we would be terribly naive to assume it could not happen in the U.S. or Western Europe.

IS THE NEW AGE MOVEMENT REALLY A THREAT TO CHRISTIANS?

Ardent New Agers see the Church as a backward institution that encourages men and women to remain in a state of lower consciousness. Christianity is the "heavy" in Western culture because, under Christian influence, man can only be an inferior species, a pale shadow of what he could be with the help of science. New Agers recognize that their plans to subvert and destroy biblical Christianity and replace it with an ideology based on supposed scientific laws and Eastern mysticism can best be achieved by a large number of separate organizations. Many of these organizations can be best described as cults. Some include the word *church* in their formal titles. But not all of these New Age organizations call themselves churches, nor are all New Agers affiliated with recognized cults. In fact, many New Agers vehemently object to outsiders' characterizations of their efforts as religious in scope. They protest that *their* group exists only to promote radical change in a particular segment of society, such as medicine, law, education, or government.

Some New Age groups contend their organizations are totally independent. Indeed, a few even reject the New Age label, preferring such euphemisms as the Human Potential Movement, Consciousness Movement, Holistic Movement, Whole Earth, East/West, Unity, and so forth. Structurally, their claims of autonomy are accurate, for there is no one organizational hierarchy or any document or statement of belief that unites all such groups. Yet, considering the broad aims of the New Age movement and the characteristics common to the New Age religion and philosophy, it is difficult to deny that most of the groups alleged to be autonomous are, in fact, integral components of an apparatus opposed to biblical Christianity.

Although many New Agers derive great satisfaction in identifying their movement as a conspiracy, some groups considered to be New Age in thought or action do not fit the classical definition of being conspiratorial. They operate in the open, actively recruit new members, and mince no words in stating their vigorous opposition to Christian concepts and in announcing their aims and intentions. Christians opposed to the New Age movement should not, therefore, concern themselves with whether or not a conspiracy exists. More profitable would be the Christian's forceful and firm opposition to New Age beliefs and activities, no matter what organization, group, or individual is involved.

ULTIMATELY, THERE IS ATHEISM

The New Age believer cannot bring himself to admit there must be a first cause, a grand Creator separate and apart from his magnificent creative efforts. Though he may continue to use the word *God*, the New Age believer is no more than an atheist in a new, more sophisticated form. New Age man, in order to lift himself up as a deity, finds it necessary to bring God down from his abode in the high places and make him into little more than a collection of inanimate material and endlessly active subatomic particles. By removing God from his throne, the New Ager believes man will become the powerful master of his own destiny, maker of his own dreams: God incarnate. He does not realize that with God all things are possible, but without God, Satan inevitably moves in to fill the gap. Seeking autonomy, man finds fetters. Seeking lordship, he becomes a slave.

CHAPTER NOTES

PREFACE

1. Julian Huxley, *Religion without Revelation* (London: Max Parrish, 1959).

CHAPTER 1   Who Needs God?

1. V. Gordon Childe, *Man Makes Himself* (London: Pitman, 1936; revised 1941 and 1951; New York: New American Library, 1983).

2. Elizabeth C. Hirschman. Quoted in "1984: Fact or Fiction?" *New York University Business,* Fall 1983/Winter 1984, p. 45.

3. Ashley Montagu and Floyd Matson, *The Dehumanization of Man* (New York: McGraw-Hill, 1984).

4. Michael Saloman, *Future Life* (New York: Macmillan, 1983).

CHAPTER 2   Man the Creator: Robotics and Bioengineering

1. Neil Frude, *The Intimate Machine: Close Encounters with Computers and Robots* (New York: New American Library, 1983).

2. *Biochips and Biosensors: Technology Assessments, Business Opportunities, and Market Forecasts to 1995 and Beyond* (Gorham, Maine: Gorham International, Inc., November 1984).

3. Geoff Simons, *Are Computers Alive?* (Boston: Birkhauser, 1983).

4. Robert Freitas, Jr., "Self-replicating Robots," *Omni*, July 1983, p. 44.

5. Texe W. Marrs and Wanda J. Marrs. *Robotica: The Whole Universe Catalogue of Robots* (Briarcliff Manor, N.Y.: Stein and Day, 1987).

6. Joseph Deken, *Silico Sapiens: The Fundamentals and Future of Robotics* (New York: Bantam, 1985).

7. Joseph Weizenbaum, *Computer Power and Human Reason* (San Francisco: W. H. Freeman, 1976).

8. G. Harry Stine, *The Silicon Gods* (New York: Dell, 1984). Also see David Ritchie, *The Binary Brain: Artificial Intelligence in the Age of Electronics* (Boston: Little, Brown, 1984).

9. Arthur C. Clarke, *Profiles of the Future* (New York: Holt, Rinehart, & Winston, 1984).

10. Albert Rosenfeld, *The Second Genesis: The Coming Control of Life* (New York: Vintage, 1975).

11. Deken, *Silico Sapiens.*

12. Frank Tipler, quoted in "Perfect Timing: In a Universe of Ten Billion Galaxies, Why Did Intelligent Life Hit This Particular Planet?" *New Age Journal*, December 1985.

13. Jean Rostrand, *Can Man Be Modified?* (New York: Basic Books, 1959).

14. Kathleen Sullivan, "Technology of Butterflies," *Austin American-Statesman*, October 14, 1985, p. D1.

15. Jeremy Rifkin. *Algeny* (New York: Viking, 1983).

16. Carl Sagan, quoted in *U.S.A. Today*, October 11, 1985.

17. See Stuart Litvak and A. Wayne Senzee, *Toward a New Brain: Evolution and the Human Mind* (Englewood

Cliffs, N.J.: Prentice-Hall, 1986). See especially pp. 194–202.

18. Edward Cornish, "Deciding Our Own Evolution," *The Futurist*, October 1985.

19. Richard Dawkins, *The Selfish Gene* (New York: Oxford University Press, 1976), p. 215.

CHAPTER 3   A Global Brain for Mankind: Computers

1. Jacques Vallee, *The Network Revolution* (Berkeley, Calif.: And/Or Press, 1982).

2. David Burnham, *The Rise of the Computer State* (New York: Random House, 1983).

3. David Foster, *The Intelligent Universe: A Cybernetic Philosophy* (New York: G. P. Putnam, 1975), pp. 16-17. Foster's theories possibly are built on the earlier ideas of Nikola Tesla, the genius who invented the alternating current electrical generating system. For example, see John J. O'Neill's *Prodigal Genius: The Life of Nikola Tesla* (Hollywood, Calif.: Angriff Press), p. 251.

4. Foster, *Intelligent Universe*, p. 98.

5. H. D. Corvey and Neil McAlister, *Computer Consciousness: Surviving the Automated 80s* (Reading, Mass.: Addison-Wesley, 1980), p. 7.

6. A. E. Wilder Smith, *The Creation of Life* (Wheaton, Ill.: Harold Shaw, 1970; Master Books/CLP Publishers, 1981).

CHAPTER 4   States of Chemical Bliss: Mind-altering Drugs

1. Jonathan Glover, *What Sort of People Should There Be?* (New York: Penguin, 1984).

2. V. I. Chernyshoy, quoted in John Barron, *KGB Today: The Hidden Hand* (Pleasantville, N.Y.: Reader's Digest Press, 1974).

3. Marilyn Ferguson, *The Aquarian Conspiracy: Personal*

and Social Transformation in the 1980s (Los Angeles: J. P. Tarcher, 1980), p. 89. Also see pp. 90-97.

4. Ibid.

5. Ibid, p. 375.

CHAPTER 5 Tech Tools for the Antichrist: Systems of Surveillance and Control

1. Senator William Cohen, quoted by David Burnham, "Computer 'Dossiers' Are Arousing Concern Over Privacy Invasion," *New York Times Service*, June 11, 1984.

2. Russell Targ and Keith Harary, *The Mind Race* (New York: Random House, 1984), p. 45.

3. Glover, *What Sort of People*, p. 167.

4. Stine, *Silicon Gods*, pp. 201-254.

5. Julie Ann Miller, "Chips on the Old Block," *Science News*, June 28, 1986, pp. 408-409.

6. Stine, *Silicon Gods*, p. 216.

CHAPTER 6 The Weapons and Warriors of Armageddon

1. Billy Graham, *Approaching Hoofbeats: The Four Horsemen of the Apocalypse* (Waco, Tex.: Word, 1983).

CHAPTER 7 The Horrible Prospect: Nuclear War

1. William J. Koenig, *Weapons of World War III* (London: Bison Books, 1983).

2. Albert Einstein, quoted in the foreword to Charles Hapgood, *The Path of the Pole* (Radnor, Penn.: Chilton, 1970).

CHAPTER 8 Terror from the Heavens: Space and Air Warfare

1. U.S. Air Force, Department of Defense, *Report to the 98th Congress of the United States of America* (Washington, D.C.: Government Printing Office).

2. Allan Maurer, *Lasers: The Light Wave of the Future* (New York: Arco Publishing, 1982). Also, see Cliff Laurence, *The Laser Book: A New Technology of Light* (New York: Prentice-Hall, 1986).

3. See *Beam Defense: An Alternative to Nuclear Destruction* (Fallbrook, Cal.: Aero Publishers, 1983). Authored by experts with the Fusion Energy Foundation, this book discusses a Soviet device that generates laser pulses of 300 billion watts, the downing of missiles in Soviet laser weapon tests, and new Soviet land-based laser systems capable of destroying or disabling aircraft and satellites.

4. U.S. Air Force, *Report*.

CHAPTER 9 Invisible Agents of Death: Chemical and Biological Warfare

1. Sterling Seagrave, *Yellow Rain: A Journey Through the Terror of Chemical Warfare* (New York: M. Evans, 1981). Also see "Tiptoe Through the Toxins," *Wall Street Journal,* December 1, 1982; Barry Wain, "Refugee Camp Doctor Claims UN Team Misunderstood Yellow Rain Controversy," *Wall Street Journal,* October 15, 1982; and William Kucewicz, "Mycotoxins: The Scientific Battlefield," *Wall Street Journal,* May 30, 1984. For a more recent report on the use of "liquid fire, yellow rain, and other outlawed munitions" by the Soviet Union against Afghanistan freedom fighters, see Daniel Dravot, "Weapons of Terror," *International Combat Arms,* March 1985, p. 73.

2. Jeremy Paxman and Robert Harris, *A Higher Form of Killing: The Secret Story of Gas and Germ Warfare* (New York: Hill & Wang, 1982).

3. Soloman Snyder, quoted by Richard F. Harris, "Scientists Testing Revolutionary Drugs," Scripps-Howard News Service, November 7, 1985.

4. James Dunnigan, *How to Make War* (New York: William Morrow, 1982), pp. 266-286.

CHAPTER 10   No Place to Hide: The War Below

1. Donald Latham, quoted in Lance Gay, "Supercomputers to Make Warriors Better Informed, Deadlier," Scripps-Howard News Service, November 17, 1982.

2. Frank Verderame, quoted by Russell Mitchell, "Robot Soldiers Being Perfected," *Austin American-Statesman*, June 25, 1984, p. E2.

3. Frank Gavin, "Robots Go to War," *International Combat Arms*, July 1985, pp. 14-23.

4. In 1974, at a conference held by the respected Institute of Electrical and Electronic Engineers (IEEE), James Beal, an aerospace engineer and researcher with Martin-Marietta Corporation, described the potential impact of bioelectronic weapons as "staggering." The space engineer also warned of Soviet advances in this field. Beale's paper was entitled, "Field Effects, Known and Unknown, Associated with Living Systems."

CHAPTER 11   Brain Invaders: Psychic Warfare

1. Targ and Harary, *The Mind Race*.

2. Ibid., pp. 263-276. Also see the report, *Soviet and Czechoslovakia Parapsychology Research* (Washington, D.C.: Defense Intelligence Agency, 1975).

3. *Research into Psi Phenomena: Current Status and Trends of Congressional Concerns* (Washington, D.C.: Congressional Research Service, 1983).

4. *Survey of Science and Technology Issues: Present and Future* (Washington, D.C.: Committee on Science and Technology, U.S. House of Representatives, 1981). For additional information on psychic warfare research, see Edith Roosevelt "Psychic Warfare," *International Combat Arms*, May 1985, pp. 76-81.

CHAPTER 12   The World Powder Keg: Why War Prevails

1. Nigel Calder, *1984 and Beyond* (New York: Viking, 1984).

2. Mary Craig, *Six Modern Martyrs* (New York: Cross-road Books, 1985).

3. Two particularly poignant accounts of the Cambodian holocaust were the book, *Murder of a Gentle Land: The Untold Story of a Communist Genocide in Cambodia,* by John Barron and Anthony Paul (Pleasantville, N.Y.: Reader's Digest Press, 1977) and the Academy Award-winning movie, *The Killing Fields.*

4. Alexander Solzhenitsyn. Reported by David Millward, Independent Press Service, London, May 11, 1983.

5. Koenig, *The Weapons of World War III.*

6. Lt. Col. John F. Guilmartin, "The Fifth Horseman," *Air University Review,* May-June, 1982.

CHAPTER 13 Flashpoint: The Middle East

1. This statement by President Ronald Reagan was reported in the Associated Press, *Time,* and *Newsweek,* and widely reported in many other media.

2. Pentagon and Defense Department officials continue to warn that the Soviet Union has a decisive advantage in conventional arms and leads the U.S. in many strategic capabilities as well. See *Soviet Military Power* (Washington, D.C.: Department of Defense, 1985) and USAF FY 85 *Report to the 98th Congress of the United States of America* (Washington, D.C.: USAF).

3. Richard M. Nixon, *The Real War* (New York, Warner Books, 1981).

4. Israel economic statistics and facts compiled from "Israeli Technology Today" and other reports and press releases issued by the Consulate General of Israel, New York and Washington, D.C.

5. Gen. E. C. Meyer, quoted by Maj. Gen. Henry Mohr, "The Kremlin's March toward World Domination," *St. Louis Globe-Democrat,* April 13, 1982, p. A8.

6. For an analysis of the Carter Doctrine, see "U.S. Interests and Regional Security in the Middle East," by Paul Jab-

ber, assistant professor of political science, University of California at Los Angeles, *Daedalus,* Fall 1980, pp. 67-80.

7. Steven R. Weisman. "Reagan Says U.S. Wouldn't Allow Saudi Takeover Endangering Oil," *New York Times,* October 2, 1981, p. 1.

CHAPTER 14   The Soviet Union: Military Giant, Economic Dwarf

1. Russia's declining oil reserves and resulting economic problems have been well documented in the U.S. and foreign press. For example, see "Soviets Struggling to Maintain Oil Output," by Leonard Silk, *Houston Chronicle,* June 9, 1985, p. 16, sec. 4. Even the Soviet press now admits the oil shortage (Moscow's *Socialist Industry,* January 1986).

2. Caspar Weinberger, quoted by George Wilson, "U.S. Urges Allies to Aid in Defense of Persian Gulf," *Washington Post,* October 23, 1981, p. 26.

3. Chairman of the Joint Chiefs of Staff, *U.S. Military Posture for FY 1982* (Washington, D.C.: U.S. Department of Defense, 1982).

4. Lt. Gen. P. X. Kelley, quoted in "A Year After—New U.S. Role in Mideast," *U.S. News and World Report,* November 3, 1980, p. 39.

5. Gen. Robert Mathis. Quoted by Larry Levy, "U.S. Air Force Best General Says," *Tulsa Tribune,* February 6, 1982, p. 5.

6. Adm. Thomas Hayward, "U.S. Navy: No More Margin of Comfort," *Christian Science Monitor,* March 31, 1981, p. 26.

7. Adm. Elmo Zumwalt, "Naval Battles We Could Lose," *International Security Review,* Vol. 16, No. 2, Summer 1981, p. 139-156.

8. Gen. Maj. N. Sushko and Col. S. A. Tyushkevicha, *Marxism-Leninism on War* (Moscow: Voenizdat, 1965), p. 366.

9. Richard Foster, "On Prolonged Nuclear War," *International Security Review,* Vol. 6, No. 4, Winter 1981-82.

CHAPTER 15   The New Military Powers: Europe, China, and Japan

1. France's post-WW II leaders have consistently taken an independent stance. In the 1960s, Charles de Gaulle forced the United States to close its military bases on French soil. More recently, on July 7, 1986, French President Francois Mitterand, in a public toast to visiting Soviet leader Mikhail Gorbachev, declared, "It is time for Europeans to become masters of their own destiny" (Associated Press, July 8, 1986).

2. Thomas Ainlay, Jr., "Japan's Shogun Fever," *Asia Week,* June 10, 1983.

3. Robert Christopher, *The Japanese Mind: The Goliath Explained* (New York: Ballantine, 1984).

4. Russell Braddon, *Japan against the World: 1941-2041: The One Hundred Year War for Supremacy* (New York: Stein and Day, 1983).

5. Harold Hakwon Sunoo, *Japanese Militarism: Past and Present* (Chicago: Nelson-Hall, 1981).

APPENDIX II   The New Age Movement: A Scientific Religion for the End Time?

1. Lola Davis, *Toward a World Religion for the New Age* (Farmingdale, N.Y.: Coleman Publishing, 1983).

2. Fritjof Capra, *The Tao of Physics,* 2nd edition (New York: Bantam, 1984).

3. Bob Toben and Fred Alan Wolf, *Space Time and Beyond* (New York: Bantam, 1984).

4. David Foster, *The Intelligent Universe.*

5. Heinz R. Pagels, *The Cosmic Code: Quantum Physics and the Language of Physics* (New York: Simon and Schuster, 1982).

6. Charles Lumden. Quoted by Andrea Dorfman, "How Did Apes Lead to Man?" *Science Digest*, October 1985.

7. Ruth Montgomery, *Threshold to Tomorrow* (New York: G. P. Putnam, 1982).

BIBLIOGRAPHY

In addition to the references in the text and notes, listed below are many of the resources used by the author. Readers who wish to study further may refer to these sources.

PART I

Bowler, Peter J. *The Eclipse of Darwinism*. Baltimore: Johns Hopkins University Press, 1983.

Briggs, John P., and David F. Peal. *The Looking Glass Universe*. New York: Simon and Schuster, 1984.

Capra, Fritjof. *The Turning Point*. New York: Simon and Schuster, 1982.

Davies, Owen, ed. *The Omni Book of Computers and Robots*. New York: Zebra Books, 1983.

Denton, Michael. *Evolution: A Theory in Crisis*. Washington, D.C.: Adler and Adler, 1986.

Feigenbaum, Edward A., and Pamela McCorduck. *The Fifth Generation: Artificial Intelligence and Japan's Computer Challenge to the World*. Reading, Mass.: Addison-Wesley, 1983.

Gammon, Roland. "Scientific Mysticism." *New Realities*, December 1980.

Goodavage, Joseph F. *Magic: Science of the Future*. New York: New American Library, 1976.

Gross, Martin L. *The Psychological Society*. New York: Simon and Schuster, 1978.

Grove, J. W. "Rationality at Risk: Science against Pseudoscience." *Minerva*, Summer 1985.

Hoyle, Fred. *The Intelligent Universe*. New York: Holt, Rinehart, and Winston, 1984.

Jantsch, Eric. *The Self-organizing Universe*. New York: Pergamon, 1980.

Jastrow, Robert. *God and the Astronomers*. New York: Warner Books, 1980.

Kahn, Carol. *Beyond the Helix: DNA and the Quest for Longevity*. New York: Times Books, 1985.

Krimsky, Sheldon. *Genetic Alchemy*. Cambridge, Mass.: MIT Press, 1985.

LeShan, Lawrence. *The Medium, the Mystic, and the Physicist*. New York: Ballantine, 1975.

Litvak, Stuart, and A. Wayne Senzee. *Toward a New Brain*. Englewood Cliffs, N.J.: Prentice-Hall, 1986.

Logsden, Tom. *The Robot Revolution*. New York: Simon and Schuster, 1984.

Marrs, Texe W. *The Personal Robot Book*. Blue Summit Ridge, Penn.: TAB Books, 1985.

Restak, Richard M. *The Brain: The Last Frontier*. New York: Doubleday, 1979.

Roszak, Theodore. *Person/Planet*. New York: Doubleday, 1976.

Sagan, Carl. *The Dragons of Eden*. New York: Random House, 1977.

"Science Contra Darwin: Evolution's Founding Father Comes under New Attack." *Newsweek*, April 8, 1985.

Smith, R. Jeffrey. "The Dark Side of Biotechnology." *Science*, Vol. 224.

Stableford, Brian. *Future Man: Brave New World or Genetic Nightmare?* New York: Crown, 1984.

Stalker, Douglas, and Clark Glymour, eds. *Examining Holistic Medicine*. Buffalo: Prometheus, 1985.

Stine, G. Harry. *The Hopeful Future*. New York: Macmillan, 1983.

Sylvester, Edward J., and Lynn C. Klotz. *The Gene Age*. New York: Scribner's, 1983.

Taubes, Gary. "An Electrifying Possibility." *Discover*, April 1986.

Young, Arthur M. *The Reflective Universe*. New York: Delacorte, 1976.

Yulsman, Tom. "The Evolution Express: Galapagos Study Shows That Species Evolve with Surprising Speed." *Science Digest*, October 1985.

Zimmerman, Burke K. *Biofuture: Confronting the Genetic Era*. New York: Plenum, 1984.

PART II

Adelson, Edward. "Space Weapons: The Science behind the Big Debate." *Popular Science*, July 1984.

"Air Force Mission in Space." *Fact Sheet*, U.S. Air Force, Office of Public Affairs, Washington, D.C.

"Army Devising New Air Defense Weapons." *Air Force Times*, August 20, 1984.

"Army Testing Robots for Some Combat Jobs," *SAM*, January 1983.

Bonds, Ray, ed. *The U.S. War Machine*. New York: Crown, 1983.

Brady, Michael, and Lester Gerhardt. *NATO Advanced Study Institute on Robotics and Artificial Intelligence*. New York: Springer-Verlag, 1984.

Brodie, Milton. "21st Century Soldier." *International Combat Arms*, March 1985.

Cady, Steven E. "Beam Weapons in Space: A Reality We Must Confront." *Air University Review*, May-June 1982.

"Chemical Warfare—Special Report." *World Press Review*, June 1984.

Cunningham, Ann, and Mariana Fitzpatrick. *Future Fire: Weapons for the Apocalypse*. New York: Warner Books, 1983.

Davis, Dwight. "Assessing the Strategic Computing Initiative." *High Technology*, April 1985.

Dravot, Daniel. "Weapons of Terror: Soviet Chemicals and Explosives in Afghanistan." *International Combat Arms*, March 1985.

Garvey, Charles, and James Richardson. "Robot Warrior." *Robotics Tomorrow Newsletter*, Vol. 2, No. 3, October 1985.

Gavin, Franc. "Robots Go to War." *International Combat Arms*, July 1985.

Heppenheimer, T. A. "Zapping Missiles in Space." *High Technology*, August 1985.

Kaplan, H. R. "Space—The New Military Dimension." *Sergeants*, March 1983.

Karas, Thomas. *The New High Ground*. New York: Simon and Schuster, 1983.

"Killer Electronic Technology." *Business Week*, September 20, 1982.

Kinnucan, Paul. "Superfighters." *High Technology*, April 1984.

Middleton, Drew. "Army Supertank Ushers in the New Era of Combat." New York Times Service, December 15, 1985.

Miller, Charles A. "The Design War behind the Army's Superchoppers." *Popular Science*, February 1984.

Poyer, Joe. "Soviet Military Power 1985." *International Combat Arms*, September 1985.

Roosevelt, Edith K. "Psychic Warfare." *International Combat Arms*, May 1985.

"Space War Era—It's Already Here." *U.S. News and World Report*, December 17, 1984.

Tucker, Jonathan. "Military DNA Research Stirs Debate." *High Technology*, July 1984.

U.S. Air Force, Department of Defense. *USAF FY85 Report to the 98th Congress of the United States of America.* Washington, D.C.: Government Printing Office.

PART III

Davidson, William H. *The Amazing Race: Winning the Technorivalry with Japan.* New York: John Wiley, 1984.

Dyson, Freeman. *Weapons and Hope.* New York: Harper and Row, 1984.

Getler, Michael. "Joint Chiefs of Staff Offer Gloomy View of Power Balance." *Washington Post,* February 10, 1982.

Goldman, Marshall. *USSR in Crisis.* New York: Norton, 1983.

Gutis, Philip S. "Peking Welcomes Madison Avenue." *New York Times Service,* January 2, 1986.

Hempstone, Smith. "Carter Doctrine on Safety of Persian Gulf Toothless." *Daily Oklahoman,* March 26, 1981.

Hoyt, Edwin P. *The Militarists: The Rise of Japanese Militarism Since World War II.* New York: Donald I. Fine, 1985.

Hsu, Immanuel C. Y., *China without Mao: The Search for a New Order.* New York: Oxford University Press, 1982.

Lu, Cary. "China's Emerging Micro Industry." *High Technology,* March 1985.

Massberg, Walter S. "NATO Chief Warns of New Soviet Strategy to Deny the West Use of Its Nuclear Punch." *Wall Street Journal,* October 15, 1982.

"Rearming Japan." *Business Week,* March 14, 1983.

Ritchie, David. *Space War.* New York: Atheneum, 1982.

Rousset, David. *The Crisis in the Soviet System.* New York: Schocken, 1983.

Shipler, David. *Russia: Broken Idols, Solemn Dreams.* New York: Times Books, 1983.

Smith, Thomas B. *The Other Establishment: An In-depth Study of What Life Is Really Like in Communist-controlled Countries.* Chicago: Regnery Gateway, 1984.

"Soviet Missiles Aimed toward Asia," Associated Press. *Austin American-Statesman*, January 16, 1986.

"Space: Japan Joins the Race." *World Press Review*, March 1985.

Weisman, Steven. "Reagan Says U.S. Wouldn't Allow Saudi Takeover Endangering Oil." *New York Times*, October 2, 1981.

Wilson, George C. "Persian Gulf Oil Region Near Top of U.S. Defense Priority List." *Washington Post*, June 2, 1982.

APPENDIX I: Does the Bible Prophesy a Military Armageddon?

Lindsey, Hal. *The Late Great Planet Earth*. Grand Rapids: Zondervan, 1970.

Walker, Robert. "Is Biblical Prophecy Being Fulfilled? Interview with Pat Robertson." *Christian Life*, November 1981.

Webber, David. *God's Timetable for the 1980s*. Shreveport, La.: Huntington House, 1984.

APPENDIX II: The New Age Movement: A Scientific Religion for the End Time?

Christian-oriented Books and Articles

Albrecht, Mark. *Reincarnation: A Christian Appraisal*. Downers Grove, Ill.: InterVarsity Press, 1982.

Boa, Kenneth. *Cults, World Religions, and You*. Wheaton, Ill.: Victor, 1977.

Bobgan, Martin, and Deidre Bobgan. *Hypnosis and the Christian*. Minneapolis: Bethany House, 1984.

———. *The Psychological Way, The Spiritual Way*. Minneapolis: Bethany Fellowship, 1978.

Cumbey, Constance. *The Hidden Dangers of the Rainbow*. Shreveport, La.: Huntington House, 1983.

————. *A Planned Deception: The Staging of a New Age Messiah*. East Detroit, Mich.: Pointe Publishers, 1985.

DeHann, M. R. *Genesis and Evolution*. Grand Rapids: Zondervan, 1962.

DeVries, John. "Pagan Surge in America." *The Banner*, July 29, 1985. (Reprinted in *The Christian Reader*, January-February 1986.)

"Empowering the Self: A Look at the Human Potential Movement." *Spiritual Counterfeits Journal*, Winter 1981-82.

Groothius, Douglas. "The New Age Wave: New Age or Ancient Error?" *Moody Monthly*, February 1985. (Reprinted in *The Christian Reader*, January-February 1986.)

————. *Unmasking the New Age*. Downers Grove, Ill.: InterVarsity Press, 1986.

Guinness, Os. *The Dust of Death*. Downers Grove, Ill.: InterVarsity Press, 1973.

Hunt, Dave. *Peace, Prosperity, and the Coming Holocaust*. Eugene, Ore.: Harvest House, 1983.

Hunt, Dave, and T. A. McMahon. *The Seduction of Christianity*. Eugene, Ore.: Harvest House, 1985.

Kilpatrick, William Kirk. *Psychological Seduction*. Nashville: Thomas Nelson, 1983.

Myers, David. *The Inflated Self*. New York: Seabury Press, 1980.

North, Gary. *None Dare Call It Witchcraft*. New Rochelle, N.Y.: Arlington House, 1976.

Reisser, Paul, Teri Reisser, and John Weldon. *The Holistic Healers*. Downers Grove, Ill.: InterVarsity Press, 1983.

Sire, James. *Scripture Twisting*. Downers Grove, Ill.: InterVarsity Press, 1980.

————. *The Universe Next Door*. Downers Grove, Ill.: InterVarsity Press, 1976.

Vitz, Paul. *Psychology as Religion*. Grand Rapids: Eerdmans, 1977.

Weldon, John, and Zola Levitt. *Psychic Healing*. Chicago: Moody, 1982.

Wilson, Clifford, and John Weldon. *Occult Shock and Psychic Forces*. San Diego: Master Books, 1980.

Pro-New Age Books and Articles

Creme, Benjamin. *The Reappearance of Christ and the Masters of Wisdom*. London: Tara Press, 1980.

Davis, Lola A. *Toward a World Religion for the New Age*. Farmingdale, N.Y.: Coleman, 1983.

Ditfurth, Hoimar. *The Origins of Life*. San Francisco: Harper and Row, 1983.

Fox, Matthew. *Whee! We, Wee All the Way Home: A Guide to a Sensual, Prophetic Spirituality*. Santa Fe, N.M.: Bedar, 1981.

Keys, Donald. *Earth at Omega: Passage to Planetization*. Brookline Village, Mass.: Branden, 1982.

King, Ursula. *Toward a New Mysticism*. New York: Seabury, 1981.

McWaters, Barry. *Conscious Evolution*. Los Angeles: New Age, 1981.

Montgomery, Ruth. *Ruth Montgomery: Herald of the New Age*. New York: Doubleday, 1986.

Ouspensky, P. D. *The Psychology of Man's Possible Evolution*. New York: Random House, 1973.

Price, John Randolph. *The Planetary Commission*. Austin: Quartus Foundation for Spiritual Research, 1984.

_____. *The Super Beings*. Austin: Quartus Foundation for Spiritual Research, 1981.

Prophet, Mark. "Expanding the Mind." *The Coming Revolution*, Summer 1986.

Russell, Peter. *The Global Brain*. Los Angeles: J. P. Tarcher, 1983.

Samples, Bob. *Mind of Our Mother*. New York: Addison-Wesley, 1981.

Spangler, David. *Reflections on the Christ*. Findhorn, Scotland: Findhorn, 1978.

————. *Revelation: The Birth of a New Age*. Middleton, Wis.: Lorain, 1976.

Starhawk. *The Spiral Dance: A Rebirth of the Ancient Religion of the Great Goddess*. San Francisco: Harper and Row, 1979.

Timms, Moira. *Prophecies and Predictions: Everyone's Guide to the Coming Changes*. Santa Cruz, Calif.: Unity Press, 1980.

White, John. "A Course in Miracles." *Science of Mind*, March 1986.

White, Timothy. "Will the Real Shaman Please Stand Up?" *Shaman's Drum*, Winter 1985.

For More Information

Texe Marrs and Living Truth Ministries offer a newsletter about Bible prophecy, the New Age Movement, cults, the occult challenge to Christianity, and other important topics.

If you would like to receive a free copy of this newsletter or wish to have information about other books and tapes by Texe Marrs, please write to:

Texe Marrs
Living Truth Ministries
8103 Shiloh Court
Austin, TX 78745